IT ONLY SEEMS RANDOM

IT ONLY SEEMS RANDOM

By Brenn Colleen

Dark comedic stories brought to you by the pain of experience.

An unfiltered exploration into the brash realities that come with growing up in L.A.

Copyright © 2021 by Imposter Syndrome Productions, Inc.

All rights reserved.

For more information about permission to reproduce selections from this book, contact Imposter Syndrome Productions, Inc | Los Angeles, California.

Book design by Brenn Colleen
Editing by Somerset Tullius
Printed in the United States of America

For Los Angeles natives. To Los Angeles transplants.

"Word-work is sublime... because it is generative; it makes meaning that secures our difference, our human difference – the way in which we are like no other life. We die. That may be the meaning of life. But we do language. That may be the measure of our lives." —Toni Morrison

Contents

Author's Note ix

Part I - The Valley xi

Shook Ones 1

Fight Club 5

Everybody Hurts 15

Highschool Hookers 24

Some People Suck 41

Lolita Complex 53

White Men Can't Jump 64

Part II - The City

Only In L.A. 78

Laurel Canyon 83

405 South 91

The Trouble With Cool 101

America's Next Top Shooting 112

Billionaire Boys Club 120

Summertime in the LBC 131

You Know You're a Native 140

Road Rage 143

The Crazies 152

Part III - The Coast

Don't Panic, It's Organic 161

Sixty Doves 170

Horny for Likes 176

This is America 187

The Friends 195

Shit They Should've Told You 202

Acknowledgments 206

Author's Note

It will probably help if you don't confuse this narrative with an ordinary coming of age Tinsel Town tale. There is no sugar-coated regurgitation of some shit you've read before. Transplants, and tourists see LA as an imaginary place, lined with palm trees, drenched with celebrities and stardust.

[trans· plant/verb /tran(t)s ˈplant / A Person who moves to Los Angeles from out of State (or an international move) in pursuit of fame, fortune.]

A place where hearts wander and dreams go to either live or die driving overpriced cars in rush-hour traffic. The stereotypical Los Angeles that you all know and love, is no stranger to anyone, anymore. You won't find that filtered fantasy here. I've had days that make me wonder if God smokes after he fucks me. And if I don't tell you the truth about it, who will?

We've all had to endure perfect little L.A. girls, shoving their impossibly perfect little L.A. lives down our throats in every book, film, reality show, and social feed known to man, for years. And If you're anything like me, then you could use a rest.

Take a load off, this ain't that.

There's nothing to decode here. No over-romanticized rose-colored exaggerations. This is just the truth. All of it. I even left in the ugly bits that still fail to make sense. Of course, I've taken the liberty of ditching all surnames to protect the integrity of the individuals involved. This book is nothing if not a desperate attempt at rectifying the misrepresentation of growing up in L.A. through the eyes of a native.

*[**na·tive /adjective / ¹nādiv/** a person born and raised in Los Angeles that continues to reside in their place of birth. Programmed products of our environment.]*

Even when you hate it here, you love it. You need it like drugs. You need it without even realizing it. You need the cloudless summer skies and sun-drenched winter days just as much as you need the traffic and chaos. They'll be broken up with memories so magical, that they never seem truly deserved in the first place. Although, those don't last long. And between you and I, it isn't what it looks like. The good things never are. Listen, I'm not saying by any means that I'm an expert, or that I figured this city out. But what I am saying is that this town will chew you up and spit you out, and it's worth it.

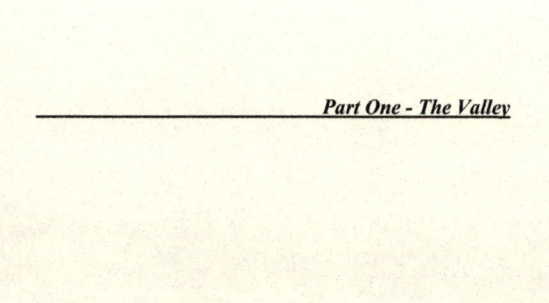

Shook Ones

"Feeling earthquakes was part of growing up, and also preparing for them: doing earthquake drills, or having earthquake supplies. The looming feeling was part of my life." -- Karen Thompson Walker

If my life were a song, The Valley would be the hook. One of those annoying one-hit-wonder hooks that you'd kill to get out of your head. Like Old Town Road or the Macarena. I lived here all my life. Until recently, I always thought of it as a bit of a drag. A shit stain of a shinier city. South of nowhere, where the smog collects like cumulus clouds. Roughly ten to fifteen degrees hotter than its metropolitan counterpart. Drag or thrill, it's, where I began, and more often than not, where I ended up. I'd be a liar to pretend otherwise.

      They say we aren't currently living in a dystopia. But who am I going to believe? Them, or my lying eyes? The city is on fire today. The sky looks apocalyptic. Ash frosts our windshields. Our throats would be sore from inhaling the smoke, but partial face coverings protect them. The masks are our only form of defense against an infectious disease plaguing the planet. It sounds like some science fiction shit, but this is real life. There's a theory that the virus originated in bats. Then again, that's just what humans are saying and the bats plead the fifth. Every square inch of this place is at the mercy of flames, viruses, and global warming. Sepia-toned pollution glazes this town as far as the eye can see, and it all brings to mind one of the most catastrophic events in my life.

When a 6.8 magnitude earthquake comes knocking it doesn't wait for you to answer. It demands its presence to be known and its fierceness to be felt. The Northridge earthquake forced us to camp in our backyard for two weeks. It was like a scene out of Day After Tomorrow as the rumble of freeways collapsing, rattling windows, car alarms and crashing concrete came suddenly at 4:31 am that January day in 1994. My dad came running into my room, scooped me up in his arms, and threw me over his shoulder in one fluid motion. My mom went to get my brother and we all went running down the hall. Luck was on our side as the water heater burst out of its closet just as we passed by. I remember my dad shielding me from the hot water explosion with his body while he shoved it back in the closet with his back. It felt like I blinked, and my family and I were sitting in the driveway in the safety of our family car. The ground continued to rumble and undulate in waves beneath us. The sound of people screaming bloody murder and crying was so loud you would have thought that their dogs had been shot in front of them.

There was a silver lining amidst the demolition; We were safe. Our house wasn't as lucky. It was a quaint one-story home on a family street. A dog made of ivy, as tall as the streetlights, stood on our corner. It's still there to this day. My mom always called it our watchdog. During the holidays, they would tie a large red bow around the neck like a collar. It would take months for the ivy to grow green and lush in the neck area once they removed it in

January. Our cute little house, on that cute block with our cute ivy puppy, was never the same. No one was. The Puppy was the only damn thing left intact.

The next few weeks had to be hell for the rest of the family, but at tens years old I remember it as more of an adventure. We pitched a few tents in our backyard and my aunt and cousin came to stay with us. Their house was decimated entirely by the land rocking the water in their pool. The only thing separating the living room and bedrooms from the pool area was a few feet and a sliding glass door that didn't do much. It was now all one wet mess.

My dad set up a generator and most of our days were spent cleaning up the remains of our home. We cooked on a hot plate and stayed warm with space heaters. We would go inside to use the bathroom, but the smell of mildew was so overwhelming that it made it nearly impossible to be in there for long. Each time a car drove by, it seemed to replicate an aftershock, quaking the foundation and our nerves. It was particularly emotional for my mom. With the loss of her family china seemed to take center stage. Looking back, my dad handled it impressively well. He's a VietNam Navy vet and tends to spring into action during high-stress situations. My brother's only despair was due to his fish tank ending up being a casualty of war. Technically, the fish were in good company. Fifty-seven deaths were reported from that all out shit show of an earthquake. All I remember losing was a few of those little gold plastic people that stood in athletic positions atop my track and field trophies.

We drove through the city to check on my Grandma Wilda. I assumed a seventy-year-old woman living alone in a house filled with antique furniture and crystal chandeliers wouldn't be in the best of spirits. Wilda lived in the hood. Like all grandmas do. Near Crenshaw and Adams close to Johnnie's Pastrami. It was a hood favorite. Smoke and debris from the earthquake playing demolition man filled the air. This was the first time that I saw that Sepia overtone all over. I rubbed my stinging eyes in hopes that it would clear up my view. It didn't. Chimneys collapsed on more homes than I could count. But I tried. I got up to sixty-one before getting bored with it. This thing shook the entire Los Angeles metropolitan area. The United States' most costly natural disaster in history.

Before the nightmare turned into reality, when other little girls were practicing kissing in their mirrors, I used to play earthquake. I'd sit with my legs crossed on the floor in front of my mirrored closet doors. Grabbing both sides of the door and begin shaking it. The reflection of the room in the mirror made it appear as if the whole room was on tilt. I'd shake until I got dizzy, then I'd put the door back on its track. It was exciting at the time. After January 17, 1994, I never played that game again.

Fight Club

"Fighting for peace is like screwing for virginity."
-- George Carlin

I've been an outsider for as long as I can remember. In Girl Scouts, none of the other troop members had any intention of playing with me. I reached that conclusion after a pigtailed blonde named Kimmy told me,

"We don't play with black girls." In her unibrow wearing defense, compassionate racism had yet to trend. Good old fashion blatant racism was still a thing, and she'd been practicing. I'd heard that line before. My cousin on my mom's side expressed similar sentiments about a year prior to girl scouts. I never had the heart to let either of them know that I prefer being biracial. They delivered the news so confidently. I hated to burst their white privilege bubble. It appeared comfortable and empowering. I could see that, even at five.

How was I supposed to figure out a way to go back in time to prevent a small-town Spanish hippie from moving to L.A., falling for a stockbroker that spotlights as a Black Panther—subsequently creating me? Damn, it sure seemed like they wanted me to figure it the fuck out or die trying. I had other shit to do. Those Thin Mints weren't going to sell themselves.

I was kicked out of the D.A.R.E. program at nine. The name was an acronym for drug abuse resistance education. Some trickle-down programs from the Reagan Era. My friend Ashlee and I got caught smoking fake cigarettes from the ice cream man behind the school bungalows with a resident pothead, David Patricka. We actually lit those bubble gum sugar sticks disguised as nicotine on fire and attempted to inhale.

Ashlee had an older sister named Solemeh, who was the coolest person I'd ever met, seen, or heard about. She was beautiful, with style to spare, and so was everyone she knew. She ditched school and had infamously hot guys over to drink beers and smoke pot by her pool. Guys so attractive they looked like they came straight off a heartthrob poster. They would watch the movie KIDS like it was their gospel, and Ashlee and I worshipped everything they did.

That eight-week educational series didn't hold a candle to the influence of Solemeh and friends. Consequences followed. The school said we were no longer eligible to graduate from D.A.R.E. My only concern was whether I was still going to be able to sing the solo at the culmination of the program. The song was Hero. You know, the Mariah Carey version of that wind beneath my wings song? Fraudulent cigarettes or not, I was the only one in our grade suited to sing that song and I'd be damned if they gave it to Shayna. She was next best, but her voice was nasally, and everyone knew it. I considered myself an artist and I was serious about my shit. Even at nine. I guess the administration agreed because they allowed the performance, which was similar to eighth grade when they said I couldn't graduate because the principal overheard me chanting two, four, six, eight you can watch me masturbate. Some bit I heard on a comedy special the night before. The school still asked that I write and sing a song at graduation. I happily obliged their request.

Accolades and traditions never meant much to me, but art and music? That meant the most. I've nearly been kicked out of every school I ever attended. Even the expensive ones that cost as much as a semester at an Ivy League College. Misunderstandings, I suppose. Sorry, Mom and Dad. What a waste.

I never told anyone about the discrepancies and brief encounters of prejudice bullshit that decorate my childhood. I'd been too black for the white kids and too white for the black kids since I was old enough to comprehend the difference. There was no grey area of multi-racial or quasi-racial. Not in the '90s. If there were, that's the cabinet that my file would be found in. The only place I belonged was with the group of people at the DMV that checked the box next to the word marked, OTHER, when applications ask us to identify our race. I'm Black, Spanish, Indigenous, English, and probably a few other races that 23 and Me has yet to divulge.

Today, the valley and the rest of the world swarm with ethnically ambiguous kids, men, women, transgenders, and everything in between. Growing up, it just wasn't that way. I guess I've always seen myself as somewhat of an underdog. It's easy to do that when you're petite and problematic. I can't remember a time when I wasn't underweight and misunderstood. So, forgive me if every misunderstanding doesn't make my priority list.

Monique was a tall skinny black chick that went to Kennedy with me. It was a school I enrolled in after being Opportunity Transferred from Chatsworth. An opportunity transfer is basically a "passive-aggressive expulsion". It's the administration kindly asking you to leave. You aren't kicked out of the district or anything permanent like that. They did, however, respectfully prefer I get the fuck out of their school sooner as opposed to later.

   My introduction to Kennedy was complicated. After a sexually traumatic start to my junior year, Monique yapping off at the mouth like a chihuahua to campaign against my existence wasn't exactly shocking. She wore plastic jewelry and enough lip gloss to shellac a wood floor. Her mouth was loud like her clothes. I hadn't met the chick a day in my life before hearing that she planned on "beating my fuck'n ass." Her words, not mine. All I knew about her was that she hung out with Britney, who was tall, pretty, and everything you expect a popular cheerleader to be, and Monique was never far behind her. Similar to that teacup dog Paris Hilton totes around. Just not as cute. There were echoes going around that she wanted to fight me in honor of her "play brother" Justin. Apparently, she heard that I was talking shit about him. The truth was far more complicated. I had no intention of setting the record straight to a stranger so sold on the lie.

   I'd never been in a scheduled fight. It all felt very "meet me at the flagpole at 3 PM" Happy Days retro shit, so I ignored the hearsay. If she wanted to fight me, then she would have to put in more effort than a game of He Said, She Said. Plus, it was Friday. I thought her desire to fight would die down over the weekend. That evening, every school in the district selected their best basketball player to play in the All-Star game. My plan was to ditch the drama and head to the game with my girl, Jenny. She and I had been tight since I left Granada.

The parking lot was packed. Every crushworthy guy in our area code was either playing or attending the game. Shane, Frank, Cliff, and Bruce. They sound like a bunch of nobodies, but their names preceded them, and they sure could wear a pair of ball shorts. All I remember from that game is that the center punched the shooting guard in the mouth so powerfully that he broke his jaw. It was wired shut for the rest of the year like Kanye West's Through the Wire. Unfortunately, the center got shipped to boarding school. I'd only seen something that graphically violent in a movie. And unbeknownst to me, things were about to get a lot more violent.

Everyone lingered in the University Parking Lot to drag out the good time once the game let out. Guys were there to meet chicks. Chicks were there to meet dudes. Numbers and casual introductions were exchanged. Bass thumping from different songs in different cars. All blasting rap music with their windows down as they made their exits from the lot. Jenny and I were walking to the car and noticed a growing crowd of kids forming behind us with every step.

Mary made her way through the crowd. I'd known her for a few years. She was one of The Cousins. A group of girls closely related, and all known for undoubtedly beating the shit out of anyone who crossed them, their friends, or their family. If you heard The Cousins were looking for you, you found them and tried to explain before they found you. Mary was ready to fight on sight no matter the occasion. She and her cousin, Lolo, had that in common. Some people saw The Cousins as problematic. I just figured they had no tolerance for bullshit and disrespect. I had them in a couple of classes at a couple of my old schools. They happen to be some of the funniest bitches I'd ever met, which goes a long way to a self-identified sarcastic girl. They weren't the only cousins that I knew. Norcole was Mary's older play-sister. Who happened to be a good friend of mine. Norcole sometimes referred to me as her "little sister." Although she has nothing to do with this story and wasn't even at the game that night. It's just that when you know three out of six cousins, you're in. My friendship with her, Mary, and Lolo earned me protection and I didn't even know it. Nor did I realize I needed it.

Mary walked right up to me and began putting my unruly curly hair in a bun while I was walking. Brushing the baby hair that framed my face back with her hands.

"Monique out here talkin shit' bout she wanna fuck you up. If y'all gon fight it's gon be a fair fight, on my momma," she said. She removed a red handkerchief from around her head, tying it around my now tight bun. Another voice came out of nowhere over my left shoulder, as a caramel complected hand reached out in front of me.

"Brenn-Brenn, take your earrings off!"

Lolo held her hand out in front of me, palm open like a small kid waiting for a surprise. I took them out and handed them to her. I wasn't sure where Jenny was at this point. She must have gotten lost in the thick of the crowd. Now when I looked behind me there was a sea of kids. I didn't know most of them. That didn't matter. A fight was a fight. Ask Pay Per View.

"You already know we ain't lettin' this bitch jump you, right?" Lolo was reassuring and struck some immediate concerns.

Jump me? Shit, that is a thing. I thought.

I now had a fundamental understanding that I was going to be fighting in front of the entire audience at the game. That was the last thing I wanted to do. The only fight I'd ever been in was with my older brother, and he's five years older than me. All our altercations would end with him restricting me in some impossible irreversible hold, and me running to tell my parents on him.

"Dad, Morgan won't stop," I'd scream.

"Take a brick from the fireplace and crack him across the head. He'll stop then,"

my dad would respond back.

He knew I wouldn't do it. But I thought about it more than a few times. I could never bring myself to do it though. Sometimes I was so mad that I wanted to and I thought if I did, that I'd kill him, and then my parents would kill me. So, I'd resort to other do-it-yourself revenge. I'd use the TV remote, a shoe, or a hairbrush as a weapon. Whatever was within reach. I figured none of that in-house experience would help me now. I was going to be in a real fight. A real fight with a girl that it seemed was no stranger to fighting. My only other experience with a school fight was with white girls at Granada. There was less punching and more hair pulling and scratching. I knew better than to consider that any source of experience.

"I been beat this stupid bitch ass, you gotta fuck her up again for me,"

Mary said as we continued to walk. I didn't know that. I also didn't know where we were going at this point. We'd passed the car three rows ago. Then we came to a stop, as Monique and three of her friends stood in front of us. Waiting to kick my ass. The parade of kids spread out into a perfect circle around us. You'd think a rap cipher or a dance battle were going to break out in the middle. It was hard to accept what was going on around me. I had yet to cultivate flexibility with my pride that would allow me to accept getting beat up in front of everyone I did and didn't know. I looked down at my shoes contemplating everything. Rookie mistake.

"If you swing on her before she's ready, we jumpin' in"

Mary told Monique.

"I told this hoe imma fuck her up and imma fuck her bitch ass up now or later,"

Monique wasn't one for beating around the bush.

Mary and Lolo stood back. It was now just me and her. She swung and I leaned back a bit. She missed. Her fingernails scraped my neck leaving three red cat scratches. A silver treble clef necklace that my aunt gave me broke around my neck and fell to the floor. It seemed like it all happened in slow motion. The charm hit my shoe and as soon as it did I lost it before it even touched the ground. My favorite aunt gave me that necklace and I hadn't taken it off since. I rushed towards Monique, grabbed her neck with my left hand, and began punching her in the face repeatedly with my right hand. If there was one thing my dad taught me about fighting it's that you don't swing once and wait for something to happen. You fucking fight. My hair tie loosened with every hit. Giving Monique the opportunity to grasp on to it like it was her life raft. That didn't bother me. I had too much hair anyway. She clawed and scratched at my chest and neck, but I didn't stop. If I did, she might've realized I could only hit with my right hand. My left was entirely useless. But that was for me to know and her not to find out. The more I punched her the more dazed she got. Unsteady on her feet. She fell onto the hood of a car. I continued swinging. She slammed her elbow into my stomach. I lost my breath for a split second. That enraged me even more. It took me back to fighting my brother. I reached out for the nearest object. In this case, it was a windshield wiper. I ripped it from the window and began hitting her repeatedly until her mouth was gushing with blood. The crowd was roaring all around us. I half expected someone to announce that the first rule of fight club is that you don't talk about fight club. It didn't last long, but it felt like forever. I didn't feel the punches when they landed on me or the blood from the scratches. When you're in the middle of a fight pain, logic and time come to a stop.

  A rush of campus security flooded the scene, and everyone scattered. I could overhear my description through their walkie-talkies. "Black female student, black curly hair in a grey shirt heading towards Zelzah." Wrong, I was running with Mary and Lolo, and had no idea where the fuck we were going but it wasn't Zelzah street. A car stopped alongside us. The driver screamed "get in", and Thank God. Jenny was nowhere to be found. Neither was a ride home. Low and behold it was Norcole and another cousin named Donita up in front. We hopped in and they took me home.

Over the weekend I got tons of calls asking me to retell the story. I told it to the best of my recollection. During the fight, it felt like it kept switching back and forth between slow motion and hyper-lapse, so it was hard to remember everything that had ensued. Monday at school the halls rang with rumors about the fight at the All-Star game.

"Y'all watch out, here comes Tyson," Mary said.

Monique was conveniently absent that day. Mary and Lolo ran up to me congratulating me on my win. I didn't even know I won because I was just trying not to lose. I tried not to smile, but I couldn't help but smirk.

Everybody Hurts

"The walls of her room are screaming out loud all of the secrets that she's held onto for all these years, every tear that broke her heart and slashed her wrist, and every memory that rips apart her soul. And to this day, she still can't breathe."
-- Anonymous

Deep in the San Fernando Valley's northwest corner, you'll find yourself in Chatsworth, California. Home of career criminal and racist cult leader, Charles Manson. The good news is that sick fuck got locked up before I was born. Fast forward a few decades, and now Chatsworth has been promoted to the valley's dirty little secret. Also known as "porn valley" or the porn capital of the world. Your choice.

    I have to admit it is borderline disturbing that the place I called home throughout my adolescence is where the majority of porn was filmed over the past two decades. Fucking on camera, fetishes, and kinks became a multibillion-dollar industry. I was ten at the time my family moved to Chatsworth. It was our means to an end after the Northridge earthquake came for our house like a bat out of hell.

    By then I was the only mixed girl in town and used to it. A general color palette of beige and peach skin tones monopolized most of the places I'd been. Blonde messy buns and hazel eyes were a hot commodity. I didn't have either. My hair is as wild and as unruly as my mouth. I'm moderately light, although I didn't find that out until I was a teenager. I always thought there were black people and not black people, and I was in the first category. The concept of shadism and all that other divisive bullshit pumped into society was news to me.

The only time I saw someone who looked remotely like me was when I'd watch T.V. or steal C.D.s from my brother's collection. I desperately obsessed over the cover booklets. Reading them front to back: every word, every credit. Hanging on every lyric. It just seemed like a better place to be, a place with infinite creativity and diversity. I spent the majority of my childhood in my room writing songs. My brother taught me how to write when I was six. Probably the most meaningful gift he's ever given me. I worshipped him as a kid, as younger siblings often do. I'd wear his hand-me-downs with pride, and we'd stay up all night with sugar highs watching Snoop Dogg's Murder Was the Case VHS over and over. He was the coolest person I ever met, and I wanted to be just like him.

In my defense, this was before his indestructible phase, where he sold his soul to the Gods of electronic music and became a Jungle D.J. This was the guy who taught me how to put scotch tape over one side of a cassette to record songs off the radio. The guy that drug Eric Cobain across the schoolyard on his face for pantsing me the first day of first grade. My hero turned biggest critic. His name's Morgan, by the way. Did I mention that? He's been an undercover computer nerd since before I was even on the scene. My mom said that when he was three, he wrote a letter to Santa Clause that read:

Dear Santa,

I want a personal computer with a graphical user interface.

If you need help, wake me up.

From, Morgan.

Today he works at some billionaire tech company in San Francisco, where the rest of the tech nazis congratulate themselves on being masters of the universe. Chatsworth was the place we went to get back on our feet, and we did. By the time high school rolled around, Morgan had skipped out on my offer to be his lifelong Protégé. His fascination with desert parties and flirtation with MDMA were no competition to sugar highs with your little sister. A rejection that would typically penetrate the surface. Not this time. I hardly had time to notice Morgan's new busy schedule.

My friend Raychel and I were busy getting ourselves into all sorts of shit which left little time to spare. She was the only other girl in our grade that didn't look like the typical Kristen, Kaitlyn, or Kimmy. Her Phillipino and German background gave her this too exotic for the suburbs aura. What I loved most about hanging with Ray is that she did everything like she'd done it before. In all fairness to her, she probably had. When we were kids, she'd run away to my house, and I'd hide her under my bed. I didn't ask too many questions. I could tell that she'd been through some shit she didn't want to relive by talking about it.

Her mom, Karen, suffered from an on again off again substance abuse addiction. When it was on, it was on. Downers would steal her self worth and uppers had her wired like a suped-up microwave. From a selfish standpoint, I thought she was a damn good time. My parents were overprotective and predictable. Not Karen. Karen was a figure it out yourself and anything goes, type of mom. I respected the difference in the parenting approach. She was also the first mom I'd ever seen wear cut off shorts. Karen was a badass, and when she wasn't fighting life, it seemed like she knew it. At Raychel's house, we could do all the things essential to being a teenager, like smoke weed and have boys over.

As trivial as it might seem today, those two little interests were at the center of our existence at sixteen. Raychel was living a life worth writing about without even realizing it. She was troubled and laidback about it with actual freedom. I wished I had a taste of that every time I came across a dandelion before blowing so hard, my cheeks would ache. "I wish I had Raychel's life" I use to whisper before the particles of the wish weed I picked went everywhere. Vicariously living through someone else isn't living at all. Not that any of this psychiatric philosophy was on my mind at the time. Ray and I just got each other. We had fun. And that was enough to keep us attached at the hip.

Standard Valley party protocol took place that summer; Someone's vacant house with a pool, valley kids tragically in search of debauchery, mixed with generous amounts of alcohol and weed made for a party. A nitrous oxide tank for a chosen few. Harder drugs, just a phone call away. And of course, rap blasted at deafening levels. Horny teenagers doing everything in their power to hookup in hopes of feeling desired, if even for just one night.

Sure, summer school broke up a lot of the raging, but even then, the school days were half days. We were free to do as we pleased by lunch. It turns out we pleased quite a bit.

I did my time at Chatsworth High. A second choice after politely being asked to leave Granada Hills. A public school that the students openly referred to as Suicide High. In my first year there, a student named Gabe tied a bunch of bricks to his feet and rolled himself off his roof into a pool. It was announced on the intercom along with counseling resources to aid grieving students. That same announcement was made a few months later when a student blew their head off, and again when another slit her wrists and had her way with her mom's medicine cabinet. Peer mediation and grief counsel were encouraged.

Enrolling in Chatsworth was a relief. I'd grown up with a decent amount of the students there. Between grade school, junior high, team sports, and camp., There were more than enough familiar faces populating the halls to make me feel at home. I'd been kicked out of so many schools throughout my educational pursuits that it was nice to finally end up around people I knew. The whole New Girl routine gets old fast. More importantly, Raychel went to Chatsworth. The old band was back together again.

She snagged the spot of head cheerleader and somehow talked me into trying out for the squad. To be clear, the last word that anyone would ever use to describe me is "peppy." I resented the idea of school pride on so many levels and for so many reasons. And it seemed to resent me back. Nevertheless, Ray bet me that I couldn't make the squad. I'd describe myself as more of a hell-raiser than a spirit-raiser, but I took her challenge as seriously as a heart attack. Two weeks later, I found myself in formation, performing an incredibly fast-paced dance routine to Missy Elliot's "Get Your Freak On." By the end of the tryout, I knew I made the squad. Predictably, I quit the next day.

Ray didn't give a shit. I don't think she expected me to see tryouts through. But that's just what we did. What one of us did, the other followed. From Children's Theatre Network to Mason Park Basketball League. Or to the underground party scene and Millenium Dance Complex as teens. If she made out with her crush on Friday, then I was determined to do the same by Saturday. When she got her tongue pierced at thirteen, I got mine at fourteen. We both dove into life head first. Together we consciously allowed ourselves to be the bad influence that the other was looking for. And we were good at it.

Not that we were exclusively rebellious. We'd ruminate for hours on the meaning of life. I'd debate that it started and stopped with perspective, and she'd always demand that the secret to it all was love. Maybe she was right. We'd write our hopes and dreams in our journals then read them aloud to each other. There were no secrets between us, we were too young for that. We yearned to belong, and with each other, we did. She'd encourage my writing, and I'd encourage her dancing, acting, or homecoming queen campaign. Which she totally bagged, by the way. We were at that age wherein hanging out together, she could escape her mom's erratic mood swings, and I could escape the house of rules and regulations that my parents insisted upon.

The summers were unbearably hot. Valley heat can only be comparable to the depths of Hell. I mean, technically, it is a desert. It takes some getting used to if you're new. We weren't. Three-digit heatwaves in the summer were expected. Followed by news anchors reporting on how every summer we break heatwave records. This particular week it was scorching. Temperatures bounced between 100 and 104 degrees. Maybe the heat got to some people. Nothing can piss you off like sweltering weather. That summer the worst thing we could possibly imagine came in with the heat.

An ordinary summer school day came to a close around lunchtime. I mobbed to Carl's Jr. to watch some random afterschool fight with about 100 other kids. Raychel went home. The fight was crazy. A boy named Landon fought this boy, Darwin. Landon was known for two things. Being Bobby Brown's son, and beating the shit out of anyone who looked at him the wrong way. I couldn't wait to fill Raychel in on the fight. Darwin's shirt was covered with blood and Landon had become our school's undefeated featherweight champion. It was a top tier tale to tell. She was going to hate that she missed it.

When I finally saw Ray, I didn't mention a word of the fight. Every punch that I planned on describing and drop of blood was now obsolete. You see, that morning Raychel and Karen got into it. That was nothing new. But instead, what Ray came home to, was her mom's pale body dangling in their bathroom shower. Lifeless and cold. I guess it was Karen's way of telling God, "You can't fire me, I quit." It had to be the heat or the agony. Reaching an indescribable and unendurable level. It had to be that.

Her funeral was held at a nearby church. My whole family attended. It's foggy from the overpour of emotions, but I vaguely remember speaking. It was brief. I wanted to fill the silence. To prove to Ray that she wasn't alone in this. She was strong. She had to be. The type of strength I've still never known.

All these years later, she's still one of the most resilient people I know. It took some trial and error. Maybe more error than trial, but she's straight edge now. I guess she hit her quota for vices. I tried to join her once, but being sober only taught me that sobriety isn't for me. Raychel's version of happily ever after ultimately became falling into a k-hole of spiritual evolution. She has a very one-with-the-earth, most likely to attend Burning Man thing going for her. And she sure can work a sound bowl.

It's interesting, isn't it? From the ages of ten to twenty, the two of us were inseparable. Now the only time we see each other is on birthdays or if we both happen to be attending a sound bath with mutual friends. Doesn't get more L.A. than running into your childhood best friend at a sound bath in Brentwood. Despite growing up side by side, we became two completely different people. Who we always were, I suppose. Maybe the cloud of uncertainty that comes with teenage angst camouflaged our differences. Either way, I'll cherish those times. All of them. Every fucking memory. Every Goddamn mistake.

I talk to Karen, sometimes. To some invisible space of air that I convince myself she occupies. We always got along. She spoke to me like she saw something in me. It made me feel important. I don't even think she did it consciously. She just did, and it mattered. When I drive by the church back in Chatsworth, I try to fill her in on her baby girl. I say stuff like. "I know you know…", and "I know you're proud…" before carrying on about Raychel's latest accomplishments. Sometimes it's a promotion. Sometimes it's a trip.

Karen left a note behind. It was addressed to Raychel's dad and only said ten words. "You better take care of her, or I'll haunt you."

Anyone who knew Karen knew not to take her threats lightly.

Highschool Hookers

"Inevitably, what we used to be, will succumb to pull of curiosity, and you will never see with virgin eyes again."
-- Missy Higgins

You may or may not have seen my freshman best friend's work in such films as Dick Loving Schoolgirls, 18 Ready and Willing, or Cum Fiesta. However, our adventures started long before she embarked on her unadulterated aspirations for the world to jerk off to.

Shannon taught me plenty of stuff throughout our short-lived friendship. Some of it she taught me intentionally, like, how to steal our parents' cars. Some, unintentionally. Like, how to give a blowjob. She wasn't all mischievous. She had a very likable personality and was the kind of conventional pretty that you'd see on TV, which goes over devastatingly well in high school. She had stick-straight, long blonde hair, striking ice blue eyes, along with charisma to spare, and the rack of a twenty-one-year-old. That combination alone regularly landed her some tall, dark, and handsome upperclassmen drooling over her. Rumors were going around that she'd just gotten out of the mental hospital before the school year started. I still don't know why, but for some reason that intrigued me. There was something mysterious and cool about someone who society couldn't figure out. She had trouble in her eyes and seemed perpetually tainted at the hand of curiosity. There was an uncertain element of surprise that made everything worth doing when we hung out. She was wild and crazy. Whatever that means. Maybe we both were.

One weekend, like many others, we got dropped off at the local mall. You know the drill, Macy's on one end, JC Penny on the other, and a food court in the middle. Chain stores with chain shit, purchased by chain people with chain money from chain jobs. We roamed around from level to level, sliding down the escalator handrails. Obviously because the freedom of not being supervised compelled us to do so. I was enlightening Shannon on a recent run-in I had with Raychel. Who I jealously discovered had just gotten her tongue pierced.

"So when she was licking her ice cream, I could totally see it," I said.

"See what?" Shannon responded monotone and uninterested.

"Her tongue ring! Are you even listening to me? Raychel got her tongue pierced!" I screeched.

I was in a bit of a panic due to witnessing one of my childhood friends out-rebelling me. It was too much to handle and I was insulted that Shannon wasn't sharing in my enthusiasm. Upon locating a pink playboy tongue ring at the jewelry kiosk, Shannon's eyes lit up and she finally added her two cents.

"My mom pierced me and Tricia's bellybuttons last week. She can do yours too." Shannon said as she picked up another tongue ring.

"We'll have to hide it from our parents," She stuck her tongue out and placed the ring in front of her tongue to examine what it would look like.

"What else is new?" I sarcastically added.

Which, in all fairness, wasn't the most accurate statement. I'd always told my parents everything for about as long as I could talk. She was right in this case. They would kill me if they caught me with a tongue piercing. I was just glad Shannon was on board.

Her mom, Linda, was more of an easygoing parent. She was an anesthesiologist that worked at some bougie plastic surgery practice. She cashed in on plenty of discounted products. Her lips were plump, her face was full of the best Botox and Juvederm money could buy, and her tits looked like she brought an issue of Playboy to work one day, and said, "I want these."

Half the girls in our fourteen and fifteen-year-old friend group had been pricked or plumped by her. And over half had their navels penetrated. Of course, I did neither because my parents did a more than adequate job of instilling fear in me. It was surprising that Linda drew the line when it came to tongue piercings. But we had to respect it. And by respecting it, I mean, we had to do it considerately, and behind her back, so she can happily live under the illusion that we respected the boundary.

Searching for parental consent in order for me to get my tongue pierced was more of a challenge. Saying that my parents are overprotective would be the understatement of the century. They continually insisted on going the extra mile to mortify me. They practiced the type of parenting where they had to speak to a friend's parents if I were to ever hang out with that friend. By the time I was in my mid-teens, I had mastered the art of determining which of my friends had "mature-sounding" voices so that they could imitate a parent and I could continue to live out my teenage dreams in peace.

Conveniently, my older brother worked at a computer store inside the mall. I made my way to his store to inform him of my latest revelation, which was to have him give consent for me to get my belly button pierced. If I told him I planned to get a tongue ring, he would have gone on a condescending rant about how I'm too young and embarrassingly impressionable. I didn't lie, but I did omit the truth. Or maybe I shapeshifted the truth into an almost lie. Which still isn't as bad as an all-out lie.

"All you have to do is say you're Dad and agree when I call," I said.

He was walking from computer station to computer station, carrying on as if he couldn't hear me at all. Not an act I'm unfamiliar with.

"I know you hear me," I whined.

I still managed to play into my "stop ignoring me" little sister role when he was around. It was frustrating, but I didn't have time to allow the frustration to get the best of me. Shannon was waiting outside, and we had a rigorous plan to execute.

"I'm pretending I don't hear you speaking because you sound like a fucking idiot," He finally broke his agonizing silence to say.

"Whatever, I'm gonna call you in like an hour, but answer," I said as I ran out of the store.

I didn't have time to react with hurt feelings because he thought I was dumb. I also knew that convincing him to go along with my plan was unlikely, which left me with one option. State my terms and bolt before he had the chance to object to them then bolt.

"Okay, ready!" I was out of breath when I caught up with Shannon.

High off of the adrenaline of doing something we shouldn't be, we were walking down Topanga Canyon with our thumbs up like we were hippies in the late '60s.

Luck was on our side when a black stretch limousine pulled over beside us. Keep in mind this is years before generic school dances provided backdrops of limo worthy events. I think I spent all of five minutes in a limo when I was in a children's theater production, and the crew hired one to take us around the block to perpetuate the idea of unrealistic expectations to a bunch of theater nerd kids.

"Where are you girls headed?" said a voice from inside the limo.

The passenger side window was closer to the sidewalk, and only partially rolled down. We could hardly make out what he said amongst the oncoming traffic.

"We're going to get our tongues pierced. Want to give us a ride?" Shannon said as she suggestively stuck her tongue out.

"Shannon." I stabbed her in the side with my elbow and said under my breath. In girl code, that meant, calm the fuck down, or what if he's a serial killer.

"I've got some time. Get in," said the man driving.

"It's just a ride and it's not like we don't need one," she grabbed my hand while opening the car door and spoke to me in the most logical tone I've ever heard her use.

As far as our parents were concerned, we were at Forever 21 or eating Cinnabon. Maybe I was just being a baby, but something didn't feel right. From where we stood, we fancied ourselves rebels. In reality, we were rebels with absolutely no cause whatsoever. Despite what Pretty Woman teaches you, it isn't every day a limo picks you up off the side of the street. Only to act as a chariot to your desired destination. A luxury we weren't too proud to take advantage of.

Shannon filled the driver in on where we were going. He resembled a much older, much more overweight version of that creepy dad on Seventh Heaven that went down for child molestation a couple years ago. She had a business card in her bag to a tattoo shop that found its way to her at some trashy valley party.

"So who do you usually drive around in this thing?" she said while spreading her arms across the big seat like she finally made it.

"Do you think the guys from Blink 182 have been in here?" She whispered to me.

Her obsession with those pop-punk hybrid white boys could only hold a candle to my teenage infatuation with Eminem.

The only reason I'm admitting this is so that you, the reader, have undeniable proof that the teenage experience can only be described as pathetic at best. That is not my opinion. That is a fundamental fact. You're Welcome.

Shannon went from an experienced hitchhiking wild child to a little girl in a matter of minutes once the thought of Blink182 came to mind. As a teenage girl, you can only safely expose your own object of obsession when someone else has stood up in their own obsession. I wasted no time.

"What if Eminem sat right where I'm sitting" I whispered.

"Do you drive rich people or famous people?" I asked—no point in beating around the bush.

"Ladies." the driver said.

"Yeah?" we responded in unison, assuming it was a precursor to him asking us a question. Our imaginations were about as off as they could be.

"No, that's who I drive. I drive women," he emphasized.

"Yeah, but who? Like Angelina Jolie," Shannon asked. Jolie's role in Girl Interrupted was the epitome of a graven image to Shannon.

"No, just hot girls." The driver said.

"Yeah, but what do they do?" I asked. He was clearly missing the point.

"Men." He responded with a smirk on his face.

Shannon started asking a million questions. Like most teenagers, she had a fascination with sex, and discussing it to oblivion fell under that fascination. It was interesting how the very same statement that repulsed me, intrigued her. The professional prostitute chauffeur, whose name we learned was Greg, was practically foaming at the mouth at Shannon's shameless interest. I could see his concupiscent expression from the rearview mirror. It was all I could do not to upchuck all over the upholstery.

"How much do they make?" she asked.

"It depends," His answers were quick and precise.

"Everything is up to her, what she does, who she does, how much she makes,"

he said.

"I mean, a guy's not going to pay as much to get a blow job as he is to have intercourse."

Greg glanced back as he spoke and I started to notice that he would make eye contact with her when he'd say something really questionable. I could see dollar signs in Shannon's eyes like she was a character in a cartoon.

I hate when people used the word intercourse. It's just a technical way of saying sex that takes two seconds longer to say than just saying sex. Besides that, the person saying it usually has this smug "I'm sophisticated for saying intercourse instead of sex" look on their face. Like it makes them smarter than those of us that simply resort to saying sex or fucking. I'd bet that Greg thought it classed up his sleazy aura, but for me, nothing could mask how obviously he was sick in the head. I figured the sooner we got to the tattoo parlor, the better. Despite his desperation, we still had a plan to execute, and I was going to go to sleep with a Goddamn barbell through my tongue. It hadn't happened yet but I could already taste it, and it tasted like victory.

"The only thing is they have to be hot, and I mean smoking hot," Greg went on.

"C'mon Shan, we don't know what time they close," I said.

I hopped out of the car quicker than I ever thought I'd exit a stretch limo. We raced up the partially rusted, partially painted stairs to the entrance. And I also made a mental note for the future, when I'd see Greg that dirtbag on To Catch a Predator. White male, late forties, pot belly, beady grey eyes filled with hidden agendas, and an ashy come-over holding on for life. Greg lit a cigarette before casually blurting out, "I'll wait out here," before the front door of the tattoo parlor closed behind us. Wait out here? For what? You got us where we're going. Beat it, you puffy penguin.

On the upside, we were fifteen and only had the capacity and attention span to deal with one problem at a time. The problem at hand was now our battle with California state law. Technically it prohibits any permanent body piercings or tattoos if you're under the age of eighteen without the permission of a consenting adult. The shop workers gave us a few forms attached to a clipboard. Asking that we provide general information. Our name, birthdate, address, in case of emergency contact, and so on. The piercer told us that we could call a relative to give consent over the phone since we were minors. There was only one option. Both my parents would drive down to the shop and take me home before grounding me for the rest of my life if they caught wind of what I was up to. Shannon didn't even try calling her older sister. She was the poster child for a goody-two-shoes. I was still uncertain about how Morgan would play it, but desperate times call for desperate measures. Or so I'm told.

The combination of possibility and hope gave me enough courage to dial his work number anyway. He picked up after one ring.

"Computer Revolution," he said in his best code-switching customer service voice.

"Hey Dad, I'm at the shop like I said earlier, rememberrrr?" I said in a sort of a slow sing-songy way.

"Dammit. I'm not doing it." I knew I was putting him in an awkward position, but it's not like it was going to kill him.

"Anyway, dad, they want to talk to you just to make sure it's okay; hold on..." I handed the phone to the piercer, let go and let God.

What was the worst that could happen? He could potentially refuse to have my back, and I'd end up unpierced and unimpressive like I already was, I'm still not sure what he said to them, but my best guess would have been, "She's fourteen, and so is her little friend; this is illegal as fuck." Morgan wasn't a man of many words. The next thing I knew, the piercer hung up the phone, patted the leather-piercing seat, and said, "you're up," looking in my direction. I didn't want to ruin my chances by asking any questions. I hopped in the chair like I did this every weekend. Which couldn't be further from the truth.

In reality, my parents made me wait until I was thirteen to get my ears pierced. I took it upon myself to numb my cartilage with an ice cube and puncture it with a sewing needle that same month, and voila, automatic edge. At least, at thirteen, it felt like edge. Somehow I felt a lot less nervous shoving a needle through my own ear in the comfort of my own bedroom to the soothing sounds of Alanis Morisette than I did in a professional tattoo and piercing facility with a licensed piercer. I sat down, and they gave me some mouthwash to swish around in my mouth. It was a lot like the dentist until I stuck my tongue out, and they drew a small dot on it with what I hoped to be a non-toxic marker.

The piercer's name was Nate, who told me to look in the mirror at where the dark purple mark was. Explaining that that's where my tongue ring was going to sit. I took their word on the positioning and shook my head yes. What the hell do I know about safe and effective piercing positions? Nate clamped the middle of my tongue and stuck an uncomfortably thick needle through it which was immediately followed by an equally thick silver barbell. He screwed the two small balls on each end of the barbell, which was more excruciating than the initial piercing. A single tear fell down my cheek. Nate did me a solid and ignored it with me before letting out a final, "You're all set, little one," I couldn't believe it. I felt like a new woman. Answering to no one. Kicking ass and taking needles. Doing what I wanted. When I wanted. In retrospect, I was another dumb valley kid chasing rebellion in all the wrong places while proving the lengths that I'll go to prove how "cool" I am, to know no bounds.

My rebellious high came to a halt when I saw Greg and his now, not so impressive, limo still parked outside. He opened the door as soon as we walked out.

"Ladies?" he said with the creepiest shit-eating grin plastered across this face.

I didn't talk much on the way back to the mall. My tongue was swollen, I was hungry, and the piercer instructed me not to eat or drink anything for the first few hours.

"Let's get a look at those piercing, girls," My tongue was in far too much pain and too sore and swollen to extend out of my mouth. Besides that, the thought of sticking my tongue out for this scumbag was the last thing on my to-do list. Luckily, Shannon's paralyzing jealousy at the fact that she had to go to school tomorrow with her tongue intact overpowered my fear.

"I didn't get it," she pouted. There was a good ten minutes of awkward silence as we continued down the boulevard. Until

"Hey, Greg! Do you think I'm smoking hot like the girls you drive?" she broke the silence with something more awkward than silence. Followed by a series of equally awkward poses that I'd seen her do before but only when she was asking me to take pictures for her boyfriend, Miller.

"I don't know, I can barely see you from back here. I'll have to come back there." He pulled over in an abandoned parking lot by a 50's diner that happened to be closed and that Shannon and I ironically used to sing karaoke at.

At this point, there was no one else. Greg opened the car door, "Can I join the party, ladies?" Ew. It was almost like he memorized a Ron Jeremy script from some sappy seventies smut scene. I rolled my eyes harder than I ever had. Shannon finally caught on to the fact that I was irritated beyond belief. Took her long enough. He situated himself in the middle of us and started rubbing both of our upper thighs. I moved his hand off my leg as soon as he touched me and repositioned myself on the other seat. As anyone in their right might would agree, I didn't want him to get his pedophile fetish hands anywhere near me. I didn't want them anywhere near Shannon either. Not that she shared that boundary. It was only a matter of seconds before she was perched shirtless between his legs on the floor of the limo. He was sitting on the seat with both hands on her breasts, with the same sort of smile on his face that a little kid has when they get away with something. He looked directly into my eyes and said,

"Did you know your best friend had a pair of tits like this?" I remained quiet.

Which didn't happen often.

"I can't believe you, Shan, you're such a slut," I couldn't help it anymore.

She was blatantly ignoring all my social cues and body language to abort the mission. To which she responded, "I'm getting paid, aren't I?"

Apparently, they discussed some sort of compensation agreement at some point. We were in over our heads. Or maybe just I was. It seemed like I was the only one who had any issue with the current situation. Fuck it, I tried to be the down for whatever best friend. But let's face it, I'm not cut out for that shit. I had to get out with or without her. I reached to open the door to exit the car, and Greg abruptly slammed it in my face,

"Where do you think you're going?" he said in a serious and aggressive tone that I hadn't heard him use before. I tried to think of something to say, anything to say.

"I need to go get some water" was all that came out. I said it scared and shocked all at the same time. It wasn't exactly a lie. My throat was dry, and my palms sweaty. I still couldn't comprehend what was happening before my actual virgin (at the time) eyes. The most scandal I'd ever been involved in was letting a boy from youth-group finger me after church. Greg handed me a mini bottle of water.

"You have to stay in here until we're finished, or else we'll get caught." He said before locking the doors.

My tongue was now swelling up triple the size, and it was getting harder to speak, harder to ignore the pain, and watching my best bud riding our ride wasn't the most pleasing visual either. Our exciting adventure turned into a nightmare. I said nothing and stared blankly out of the window. Out of the corner of my eye, I could still see Shannon's blonde hair bouncing up and down on the semi-hard shaft of this gross middle-aged man. It was the first time I'd ever seen anything like that outside of late-night Cinemax or when I stayed up to watch Real Sex on HBO. Once they were done, he gave Shannon his card and told her they could meet whenever she wanted. He also handed her all of sixty dollars. Sixty fucking dollars! I was a virgin, and even I knew that she got low-balled. Shannon put her clothes back on and asked Greg to drop us back off at the mall he picked us up near. Our parents expected us at 6 pm, and it was already 6:30.

I'd never been so happy to see my mom and dad. Not that they were happy to see me. They were pissed. They'd been waiting for me at Borders book store for an hour.

"My bad, we were in a movie." I knew that wasn't exactly what they wanted to hear, but I had to keep it short, considering that my swollen tongue was now giving me an increasingly noticeable lisp. I also thought that

"We hitchhiked to get my tongue pierced, got picked up by a limo, and Shannon fucked a middle-aged pervert" didn't really have the right ring to it.

That next school day, I felt back to my old self, but cooler because now I had a new piercing that no one else in school had. Except for the gothic kids, but they'd always been ahead of their time. My piercing bragging rights were eclipsed by Shannon's weekend sins by the time I reached "the tree", which was our designated hang out spot on campus. Most of the girls were just as impressed with the low budget business transaction as she was. After school, I noticed a very familiar looking stretch black limousine parked in the school parking lot. No fucking way. There's no way he would actually come to our school. What in the R. Kelly was going on? Is this even real life anymore?

"Okay, so Tricia, Clarissa, and Tracy are coming with us, don't tell," Shannon whispered as she came up behind me and wrapped her arm around my neck.

"I'm grounded, remember?" A casualty of being an hour late in my household.

"Oh yeah, I forgot; well if I get anything good, I'll share it with you."

"I gotta go." My dad pulled up and honked at that very minute.

While I was walking to my dad's car, I saw my friends pile into the limo. The next day they all came back laced with Northridge Fashion Centers finest. New sunglasses, new Bath and Body Works body splashes, new shoes, random shit from Victoria Secret, new Claire's accessories. They'd clearly seen an increase in income since we usually made a whole lot of nothing.

Greg began picking Shannon and several of our friends up from school regularly. What could he possibly have said? "Hey girls, I know I'm about as old as your grandpa, but can I cop a creepy feel on your still developing body when the bell rings?" He'd give them a quick twenty bucks to feel their pubescent tits. Fifty flat to suck him off and one hundred for the whole shebang. By Wednesday, 90% of chicks in our "click" were exchanging first through third base for a few bucks.

I wanted to be disappointed in them, but I wasn't. At the time, I felt more ridiculous than they did. As if there was something wrong with me for not wanting to hook up with a predatory deviant for cash. It wasn't spoken of often. In fact, very rarely did anyone bring it up. It was a dirty little secret that everyone knew better than to let travel outside of our immediate circle.

From what I know, no one ever spoke up about Greg and what he had done. . Maybe they didn't see it as wrong. We were all convinced that we were "mature for our age." Wherever he is, he got away with it, and can now live free of consequence in his mom's basement gazing at teen catalog models plastered to his walls by his rank semen when he isn't driving for Uber. Sometimes when a limo passes me on the freeway, or a group highschoolers pile into a sprinter to transport them to some annual dance, I wonder if they're all just a couple of exits away from having their innocence stolen, too.

Some People Suck

"The terror takes you. The cage is locked and the curtain drawn. Fingers dance along as blades, carving memories into your flesh that will leave scars long past being healed."
-- Amanda Steele

Justin was the type of guy that I always hated. Entirely overrated. Even his enthusiasm was sluggish. He had hypnotizingly beautiful eyes and an attitude that screamed "Fuck it!". The careless combination of attractiveness and indifference confirmed one thing and one thing only. That I was soon to be vying for his attention like every other pathetic bitch with a pussy in our area code. He wasn't the type to be bothered or the flattering kind. The Casanova of Kennedy Highschool was a man of few words. Though everything he didn't say only made me like him more. I like how he casually french-inhaled smoke and how his pants hung right below his ass—defying gravity. I like that his eyes would transition from green to hazel depending on the temperature or his mood. I liked him for every irrational reason that you could think of. Because he was uninterested in everything. Because I misinterpreted his sexual attention deficit disorder for a challenge. Because I've always been a sucker for complicating simple shit. And the universe decided that it was my time for a crash course in life experience.

    It was common knowledge that Justin was no more and no less than a hoe. He'd had his way with most of the above-average girls at school. Occasionally tarnishing his record of bedding perfect tens by drunkenly seducing an eight-point five at a random valley party. Not that I ever inquired about his promiscuity to his face. I was far too nervous ever to say anything remotely competent. I knew there were certain things I wasn't supposed to know. So I didn't ask. I was too stupid to know better. Still, I found myself in a cold dark park only a few hundred feet away from where he and his friends were raising their forty-ounce beers to celebrate another night of nothingness. As embarrassing as it sounds, I was honored to be there.

I had convinced myself that I had a leg up on the other girls at school in the race for his interest. Justin and I had already rounded first base earlier in the summer and I'd been reliving it ever since. Exaggerating and over-romanticizing the kiss in my head like I had a rewind feature in my memory. I didn't have much experience with sex. I was clueless. Unless you count bearing witness to Shannon's taxi-cab confession the year before. What was important is that I was there with him, and they weren't. So as far as I was concerned, I was in the lead, wishing and hoping I would end up the victor. My mom always told me to be careful what I wished for.

He invited me to the park in the sort of way that all little girls dream of their crush asking them out.

"You fuckin with us after this?"

he said in a way that was both confident and careless.

If he thought I was the kind of desperate broad that would take him up on that half-ass offer, he's God damn right. I'd imagined him asking me that for months. I nodded, looking up at him as if he were going to pet the top of my head and tell me, good girl. I wasn't exactly sure of what "fucking with them after this" entailed, but I was sure that whatever it was, I was down. From what I could tell, it meant that I could spend the rest of the night hanging out with Justin. Fuck the fine print. I was all in.

      His entourage typically consisted of this wannabe gang that called themselves The C.H.A.P.S. The name was an acronym for, Can't Hate A Playas Status. It was just as stupid then as it sounds now. They'd wear all orange and meet every Sunday at the same park I found myself at. Dressed like traffic cones and pretending to matter. Drinking beer and smoking black and milds. Each just as pathetic as the next. Justin wasn't only the most sought after but the youngest of the crew. Everyone called him Pooh Bear because he was that fucking adorable. Even the guys called him Pooh. Both the varsity and J.V. cheerleaders would sew him little felt Winnie the Pooh stuffed animals in home economics class. Waiting on pins and needles for him to select which girl he'd couple up with that year. They wanted it to be them. I wasn't any better. I wanted it to be me.

      The park was empty. All you could hear is chatter from the C.H.A.P.S and squeaking chains as the wind blew the swings. I followed Justin down the hill away from everybody. I would have followed him off a cliff if it meant being close to him for a few more seconds. There was an unfamiliar chill in the air, and I couldn't decipher if it was cold out or if I was so nervous that my blood wasn't circulating correctly to keep me warm. We laid down on the damp lawn. The wet blades of grass poking through my cotton shirt were irritating and itchy. It didn't matter. I was equally elated and terrified to be there. That overpowered all other sensations and thoughts. My heart was beating so hard and fast that I was sure he could hear the awkward thumping. It sounded like listening to a trip-hop set on acid. We didn't say more than ten words to each other before he began kissing me. Approximately 2.5 seconds into kissing; Or at least what felt like it, he unzipped his pants and pulled out his dick. That escalated fast. A million thoughts rushed through my mind in what had to be less than five seconds. This isn't how it's supposed to go. He forgot to brush my hair out of my face and tell me how beautiful I am. Hadn't this dickhead seen a romantic comedy?

He laid there with a look on his face that said, "it's not going to suck itself".

Despite what my stellar make-out performance eluded to, the only erect penis' I'd ever seen in the flesh had been that flabby excuse for a dick that Greg the gross driver kept tucked in his slacks. Let's be honest; they aren't the most aesthetically pleasing male organ. I'm a lot more partial to that V area below the abs that serves as both a road map and an aphrodisiac. But that's just me. For some strange reason, Justin's dick was pretty fucking nice. As nice as it could be.

The police pulled up to the park shining their flashlights and asking us to leave. Understandable. It had been closed for hours. Justin pulled his pants up in record time and helped me to my feet. It was the first and only gentlemanly thing I'd ever seen him do. You'd think the circumstance would have called for more cop trouble than what ensued, but they wanted as little to do with us as we wanted to do with them. I think it's safe to assume that they thought we were just making out. I guess we were. The cops went over to the tables where the guys were staggered and reiterated their version of, you don't have to go home, but you have to get the hell out of here.

"Pooh, we out," Justin's older brother yelled over to us.

Once Justin's brother said what it was going to be, that was that. He was our ride. His name was Matthew, and his eyes were yellow, where they were supposed to be white. Glossy, wandering, soulless eyes. I didn't think much of him. I didn't think much of any of them. Still, I wanted them to like me. Because Justin liked them, and that was enough to convince me that I gave a shit about what they thought of me. I guess everybody plays the fool sometimes.

The park was creepy but still more inviting than the C.H.A.P.S house. Wherever we went, I didn't want to end up there. That shit hole hardly looked lived in. Dirt and wild weeds stood in substitute of a front lawn. An abandoned old rusty wheelchair that doubled as the perfect home for a family of black widows was the closest thing they had to patio furniture. Inside was just as unpleasant. The cottage cheese ceiling hung low in some parts, stained from the rain over the years. I'd only been there twice, and both times were during the day. I didn't want to see that place at night. I'd been to Justin and Matthew's house once for all of five minutes. It didn't look like the kind of place that they'd live in. It was warm and welcoming. There were family pictures on the wall where the two of them looked like they were dressed up as Carlton from Fresh Prince. Maybe we'd head back there. At least it was clean and lived in. It wasn't up to me. I had zero say in where we went or what we did. Matt had the car, so Matt called the shots. He had this sort of "I do this all the time" energy about him that made me feel as insignificant to them as I probably was. So, I shut the fuck up and rode.

       All messed up with nowhere to go; we ended up at The C.H.A.P.S house. A few stragglers were there. Leftovers from the still of the night. None that I'd seen before. I mentally established that I was the hottest girl in the house. Not much of an accomplishment, but it made me feel better in the moment. A spider web clung to my face as I walked through the door. I spent the next few minutes picking pieces of web out of my lipgloss. Justin didn't notice and wouldn't have cared even if he did. He took me through a hallway into a dark room. It was the first time he held my hand. It was also the last time, not that I knew that then.

       The only indication that we were in a bedroom was the sheetless mattress thrown under a broken window. A large piece of cardboard was barely duct-taped to reduce the draft. It didn't. It was cold, and the only light source was the neighbor's sensor light that the stray cat would occasionally set off. I ignored all the red flags and the fact that remaining there could very well end up with me needing a tetanus shot. He didn't say much. It wouldn't have mattered if he did. We carried on kissing. I didn't care about the busted window or the gross mattress. I didn't even care that he kissed like he hadn't had much practice. His tongue, surfing the waves of my mouth. I could have died. The house was shitty. The bedroom was shittier. Hell, he was even shitty. But in that moment, he was mine.

Before vanishing, he mumbled something about being right back. I assumed the disappearing act was a cover so he could buy time to get condoms—a respectable task. A half-hour passed of me sitting alone, topless, and pissed off when Pop peeked his head in the room from the doorway.

"You good, baby?" I nodded.

"You sure?" I wasn't, but I still nodded.

"You don't look it." He wasn't wrong.

Sitting on a filthy mattress, hiding my naked body behind an equally nasty pillow, didn't necessarily scream, I'm good. Pop sat on the bed next to me.

"Thanks," I replied, sarcastically under my breath.

"Naw, I don't mean like that, you always look good, you just look sad or some shit." Again, he wasn't wrong. It's kind of hard to look ecstatic when you've spent the better half of your Friday night on a piss-stained mattress.

"I've had better nights," I said. Pop laughed. I never knew why they called him Pop. He wasn't older, or anyone's dad or anything. The whole time I knew him, I never heard anybody refer to him as anything else.

"I'ma do you a favor," he said.

"Oh yeah?" I inquired. Desperately hoping that the favor had everything to do with giving me a ride home.

The idea of Justin and I was dissolving and shapeshifting before my eyes. He'd been gone long enough for me to build up a mountain of resentment. Pop put his hand on my leg, gripping my thigh, and started kissing my neck like he was copying something he saw in porn. I leaned away, crab crawling towards the wall.

"Where's Justin?" I said uncomfortably. Enough was enough. Where the fuck was he? I was sick of pretending to be the 'cool girl'. The cool girl never brings up anything that a guy could interpret as 'dramatic'.

"I ain't seen that nigga in minute," he said, scooting closer. He spoke with this new seductive tone of voice that I hadn't heard him use before. There was more bass and rasp to it.

"I'm tryna turn your night around," he said.

Again, he put his hand on my thigh.

"What's up with you, baby? You think I'm ugly or something?" Guys have this innate ability to turn fabricated insecurities into manipulation seamlessly.

"Look, I'm not into it. Can you just find Justin and let him know I'm ready to go?"

I tried to be nice. And maybe he was just trying to be nice. If I were a betting bitch, I'd say that Pop was just looking to get his dick wet. But that's neither here nor there. He left without putting up too much of a fight. I had to sit through a minimal monologue about how he wanted to make me feel good, mashed up with something about not being able to help how he felt. It was all bullshit. I was reasonably certain he didn't even remember my name. Hence why he only ever referred to me as, baby. His campaign for pussy was about as transparent as Justin's. The only difference is that I already convinced myself I liked Justin. And I was too stubborn to admit that my affinity for the kid was as pointless as waiting for his return.

He finally made his way back as if nothing happened. I don't know what I was expecting—tail spinning in a vortex of teenage emotion. I wondered if he'd sent Pop in to test my loyalty—another sad, romanticized notion. You'd have to care to test someone, and caring was about as foreign to Justin as playing the stupid silent chick was to me. "You miss me?" he said, hopping on the bed next to me. "What were you even doing?" I asked. For all, I knew he was fucking some *Tijuana* prostitutes in the alley outside. It wouldn't have been far from his realm of comfort. He had no idea that my mind wandered to these unimaginable places. No clue that I was fixated on some version of him that I made up in my head. I was loyal to that version, so I saw the mission out. I let him spoon feed me irrational excuses so we could carry on as planned.

Now, this had nothing to do with him. And everything to do with the fact that every single female at school wished they were in my place. I had no intention of taking that for granted. Sad how that can inspire a complete mood change, but it did. I let him continue kissing me with that amateur tongue. He pulled my pants off and went down on me. It was the most nerve-wracking forty-five seconds of my life. I didn't have the guts to tell him that he never found my clit. I presumed that was something he could figure out in his late twenties like the rest of his gender.

He again pulled his dick out. He was proud of it, and it showed. The joke was on him. I had nothing to compare it to. It could have been the Bentley of dicks, and I wouldn't have known the difference. It was then that those four little words that all fuck boys use on a regular basis found their way to my ears, "Kiss it for me," he said as if he'd said it a thousand times before. I knew it was common decency to suck his dick. He ate me out with no hesitation. Although, now I find it offputting when men treat foreplay like a procedural checklist to get to the fucking. I started sucking his dick exactly how I'd seen Shannon do it before. My lips started to tingle. Like when your foot falls asleep. He flipped me around, bent me over with one arm, and slid a condom on with the other. So, this is Doggystyle, I thought. I heard about the position for years, but now I was actually experiencing it. Suddenly the 'you don't love me, you just love my doggy style' SnoopDogg interlude made more sense.

    After about twenty minutes of getting jackrabbit fucked, a power struggle set in. Justin was pushing my face into the stained mattress. I figured I'd close my eyes until he was done. I caught on quickly that it was more of a *him* thing than a *me* thing. But then I noticed that the hands restricting me from lifting my head were holding me down from another direction. A direction that eliminated them from being Justin's hands at all. I tried to lift my head to prove to my crazy imagination that I was losing it, but then I felt four hands shove my face back into the mattress. I felt a flaccid dick placed in the nape of my neck, flopping between it and my shoulder. The disgusting ass mattress muffled my screams.

    "Come on, baby, you know you like this nasty shit." It was Pop.

I guess Justin did send him in, but not to test my loyalty. To test how willing I was to fuck both of them. I could've sworn I failed that test. Yet, here they both were.

They didn't have to overpower me anymore to keep my head down. I didn't want to see or remember a thing. They flipped me around, and I buried my face into the bed for them. Justin kept trying to shove his dick back in my mouth, but I kept turning away, tight-lipped, like a toddler that doesn't want to eat their vegetables. I felt Pop fiddling around in my pussy and ass area, but he couldn't get hard enough to put it in. I like to think that was God looking out for me. They switched positions. Pop was sitting over my body and holding my legs open while they took turns going down on me, and playing with my pussy like it was theirs, and not mine. The next thirty seconds have been etched in my mind, and become a part of my psyche. It affects who I fuck, when I fuck, if I fuck, how I love, who I love if I love. I'll take a stab in the dark and say these dickheads had no idea the ripple effect of their little sexscapade. Their plan started and stopped with their hard-ons.

"You love this shit," one would say. And the other would add.

"Look how wet you are, you know it feels good,"

I couldn't tell the difference between their voices or their touch anymore.

One forced his half-hard dick in me while the other restrained my wrists.

Matthew interrupted with his soulless eyes and opened the door abruptly.

"Bust your nut, we out," he said. As a reminder that this is an ongoing extracurricular activity in their world.

By the time the story made its way back to school, I found out that they edited it to make themselves appear like Sex Gods and to make me look like a cum guzzling-dick addict. It hardly seemed like a believable narrative, but I was new to Kennedy High, and high schoolers can't wait to burn a scarlet letter on someone new. Besides that, I thought I deserved it. What I used to be was tainted at the hand of curiosity. My affinity for bad boys finally wrote me a check that my ass couldn't cash. I suppose I could have said something to someone, but no one wanted to hear the tale of how two of the most popular guys in school had homoerotic predatory tendencies. It doesn't roll off the tongue the same way misogyny does. I guess the lie was more interesting than the truth.

Lolita Complex

"Being sexually assaulted threw a monkey wrench in my thinking for a while." -- Rose Mcgowan

"I think choosing between men and women is like choosing between cake and ice cream. You'd be daft not to try both when there are so many different flavors." -- Björk

My friend Bexx once described Kiely as one Salvia hit away from Azelia Banks. She wasn't completely wrong. If you would've told me that my first orgasm would be at the hand of a Disney singing twink, I would have laughed in your face before explaining how wrong you are. Then you would laugh back because nothing takes the wind out of my "anti-everything-cool-girl" sail, like falling for a fuckin Pop&B singer.

    I met her when I was nineteen, and by the time I was twenty, it was as if we never even knew each other—eternal sunshine of the spotless mind type shit. It was good while it was good. We were immediately drawn to each other. Similar to crack addicts. There's no love quite like crackhead love. Somehow, they find love in a hopeless place. Between living on the streets and scoring their next hit, they find someone they can defy gravity with and crack lean, proving they have no vertebrate, into the sunset. Together. Completely ignoring the outside world. Slow dancing in the middle of rush hour traffic smacked out of their Goddamn minds.

We did a lot of shit but stayed away from hard drugs. Salvia was legal at the time. You could walk right into a smoke shop and buy it over the counter. No questions asked. Most people hadn't heard about it, but Raychel was our resident drug expert, and very little made it past her. It's basically a plant with psychoactive properties. The leaves are supposed to have opium compounds that make you see shit. Picking up a few stragglers along the way, we took the paper bag of Salvia and cherry cloves back to Archstone. It was a luxury apartment complex for the privileged and overpaid. I was neither, but Kiely was both. The cherry cloves were for her. She lived with her group members. They were predictably pretty and nice and all the things you're supposed to say about nice and pretty people. They'd politely mind their own business when we'd run through the house like a fuckin tornado.

We all sat on the floor surrounding a dark blue ice bong. Raychel said that if you smoke it out of a water-cooled device, it works better. Something about it being easier to inhale massive amounts of cool smoke over hot smoke: I took the bong in my hands while she lit the bowl. Ray always played the coach when it came to experimenting with new shit.

"Okay, close your eyes, suck, and hold it for thirty seconds." I did. I counted to thirty in my head before exhaling a cloud of smoke that floated above us. Lingering over our heads like a rain cloud. I opened my eyes and didn't say a word for thirty more seconds.

"Well, what do you see?" I could hear Kiely's voice, but I couldn't see her. All I could see was a brick wall made of ice. I knew it didn't make sense, but my eyes were playing tricks on me. This isn't possible. I told myself. I started to shiver. The ice wall muffled their laughs, but I could still hear them. I looked behind me, and there was a wall there too. That's when I realized I was in a fucking igloo.

"WHAT THE FUCK," I screamed and began kicking. Hard. I kept kicking. I could still hear them. They were dying of laughter. I continued to kick. I closed my eyes and kicked some more. I was going to kick a hole through this fucking igloo if it killed me.

"Tell us what you see," Raychel always wanted to ride the high twice.

Once, herself and once vicariously through whoever she was with. In this case, it was me. I wasn't in the mood. I couldn't believe it. I'm being held captive by potentially murderous Eskimos, and all she cares about are the effects of some stupid plant.

"Just open your eyes, and describe it," she demanded.

I didn't even realize my eyes were still closed since my kicking tantrum. I opened one. Slowly. Then, the other. Kiely and Ray were both sitting up on their knees like kindergarteners at storytime. Observing my every movement. I suddenly became a lab rat in a psychoactive science experiment. The place was exactly as I remembered it—no polar ice caps or igloos in plain sight. The candles were lit. As they always were. Moroccan style pillows hugged the window sill. As they always were.

"I don't see anything." It wasn't a lie. I didn't see anything anymore.

The glacier prison was gone. I looked down and realized that my hands were holding the ice bong the entire time and attributed my hallucination to that. At least it was logical. Raychel and Kiely had less than memorable highs before Ray dipped off back into the depths of the north valley. Leaving Kiel and me to do the usual. I imagine our relationship was what french love affairs consist of—sex, poetry, philosophy, and art.

Not many people knew. Which made it that much more intoxicating. We'd get high to enhance the high we had from being together. She had this Lolita thing about her. Sexualized by almost everyone she knew, in one way or another. I wasn't going to help much. I wanted her just as badly as everyone else. But I didn't blame myself. She was fucked up before I got there. I just wanted to make it better for the time being.

We drove down to Hidden Hills one night after deciding Studio City had nothing left to offer. We had a weed connect there with a house bigger than a school campus. Raychel and Britt came with. Britt was a dancer from downtown that we'd met at Millenium. He usually wore bedazzled trucker hats and had a thing for Janet Jackson. He had a bad habit of saying the quiet part loud. Breaking out into intricate dance routines at the peak of our high. We'd shout out choreographer's names, and he'd switch up his style of dancing to imitate them. It kept us entertained for hours. At a hotel party we threw for my birthday that year, he flipped over a table and every glass and champagne bottle on it. To this day, he insists it was in defense of Janet Jackson. Our boy, Landon, was saying that he would "fuck the shit out of her." Far too much for Britt to shoulder.

He was a trained technical dancer, and if there's one thing the dance community will risk it all for, it's Janet motherfuckin' Jackson.

Pimp Player's real name was Robert. He'd hook us up with weed and let us invite all our friends over to do whatever. We called him Pimp Player for the simple fact that he used either or both terms in every sentence. Like a hood suburban Yaya from The Sandlot. He'd call us pimps and players like it was our name.

"What's good, pimps?" was a standard greeting. Followed by

"You guys ready to get faded. This shits gonna be playeR."

He'd accentuate the E and the R. As most kids from the west coast tend to do. Maybe he thought the slang distracted from the fact that his parents had more money than God. The rumor was, they were on the President's legal defense team. Although, that was never confirmed nor denied. I think it was safe to assume he didn't have many friends. He'd go from his crib in Calabasas to Kiely's place in Studio City to my house in Porter Ranch, back to Calabasas. Only to drop us all back home at the end of the night. Ever so often, a couple guys that looked like the team water boy in high school would pop up at his house. They'd hit on us, assuming we weren't together. Saying shit like,

"Why are you guys sitting so close? Why don't you both come sit over here," while patting their lap.

Kiely liked to fuck with tools like that. Trolling strangers before trolling existed. She'd rub between my legs and lick my neck while she stared directly at them. The dweebs would be too uncomfortable to say much back. That or their last brain cell traveled from their skull to their dick heads. You'd think that sort of behavior would have tipped me off that she had a thing for me, but it didn't. I was blinded by my thing for her. I couldn't see past it. Interpreting all of her overtly seductive flirting as a figment of my imagination. We were the same, but different. Caramel complected, five-foot somethings, with tiny frames and too much personality. She had a mean streak, but never with me. She was always tender with me.

We'd do all sorts of shit at Pimp Players. The regular tradition included smoking ourselves stupid, blasting music in his oasis of a backyard, and raiding his storeroom. You call it a storeroom instead of a pantry when it's bigger than a bedroom. It looked like a fucking Costco in there. Every snack imaginable. Rice crispy treats, fruit snacks, and as much Gatorade and Capri Suns that our high little hands could carry.

On a night when our routine got dull quicker than usual, our boredom drove us back to childhood past-times.

"Let's turn off all the lights and play hiding seek." Kiely's ideas were always so stupid; they sounded fun.

"You tryna take shots first? that shit would be pimp." I had yet to hear Pimp Player talk about anything that wouldn't be pimp. There were ten of us, which felt like a good number for such a trivial game. Kiely explained the rules.

"Okay, I'll be IT first. We have to stay in the main house, no going outside, in the theater or in the tower," Pimp Players room stayed atop a tower. You'd think a Disney Princess lived up there waiting to be saved, but nope.

"Any questions?" A student body president was dying to get out of Kiely anytime a group activity called for instruction.

"Okay, I'm gonna count to 100 to give everyone enough time. The couch is safe."

Everyone besides the two of us scattered to find a hiding spot. For no other reason, but I knew she had a plan. There was this evil plan look in her eye from the second she recommended we play the game. That wasn't new. Kiely was always up to something. Hidden agendas had become her middle name.

"One, two, three, four, five, seven..." She began counting. Walking towards me.

"You, stay," she said. As if I wasn't already.

"Twenty-one, twenty-two.." She'd randomly scream out a series of numbers. By the time she got to twenty-five, she was straddling me.

"Are you nervous?" she asked. I was. I didn't dare admit it, but I was.

"I just don't know what you're doing." It was basically true. I didn't.

"Thirty-seven...thirty-eight..." she said loudly. Then

"That's the point, if you don't like it, I'll get off, but if you like it, we should probably do it more." quietly.

"Do what more?" It sounds like I'm fishing, but I was truly confused. I wasn't sure if we were doing this to freak out some of Pimp Player's nerdy friends or if she was serious. Have you ever met a girl that fucks with everyone's head just to see if they can? She was one of those. I'd seen her do it to people before and didn't want to find myself on the other side of a twisted joke.

"I've wanted to do this since the first time we hung out," she said before screaming,

"Forty-nine, fifty, fifty-one..." I was still trying to decipher whether or not she was fucking with me.

She grabbed my face, shoving her tongue in my mouth and sucking on my bottom lip. "Seventy-six, seventy-seven... do you want me to stop?" I bit my lip looking up at her. I wanted to do a lot of things at that moment. Stopping wasn't one of them. I didn't say a word.

"I thought so," she was always good at reading between the lines.

We continued making out, rolling from the couch to the floor. She'd kiss me hard and grab my face. Shoving her fingers in my mouth, down my pants, and then inside me. She's clearly done this before. That made one of us. My lack of experience didn't stop me from getting lost in the moment.

"Ninety-nine, One hundred, Ready or not here I come," she screamed. The irony wasn't lost on me.

At around three in the morning, Pimp Player sobered up enough to drive us back to Archstone. We sat in the back so we could play with each other's pussies on the way home. That game of hiding seek had our hormones running high. Both suffering from whatever the female version of blue balls is. Everyone else in the car was passed out. Without realizing that elevators have cameras in them, we kept the same energy in there. I'd never had a friend with benefits. If I'm going to, it might as well be with my best friend. Sure, it is alarming that we told a handful of people that we were sisters when they asked. Other than that minor incestuous detail, this could work.

In her bed, we were finally free. Free to act on our inhibitions. Free to finally fuck. In girl world, that just included a never-ending game of foreplay. It felt like we'd been doing this for years. Shit, maybe she had. "You know I'm in love with you, right?" I didn't see that coming. "Since when?" I asked. "You don't have to say it back," that was meant to take the pressure off. It didn't. "I don't really know what we're doing," I confessed. We carried on like that for weeks. Hooking up at every opportunity. It was fun and came and went at record speed, almost like experiencing a relationship on fast forward.

In the end, I cheated. It's as simple as that. In the beginning, it was all passionate bubble baths and fucking in the pool. In the end, it was nothing. There, we sat on the floor. Chain-Smoking blunts and waiting for this conversation to be over. She's hurt. I can understand that. Her sometimes green, sometimes hazel eyes were wet with tears. We had that in common. This hurt me as much as it hurt her. She couldn't tell. She lit a cigarette and looked at me with this dead vacant facial expression. Sometimes you can just look at someone and feel all their pain. We started in separate directions, and it's ending in separate directions. We were too different and too similar for this to have had a chance. She informed me that my friend Shawna was the one who told her I'd been seeing Eric from the gym behind her back. Fuck Shawna. They wouldn't even know each other if it weren't for me. It didn't matter anyway. What's done cannot be undone. There's no romantic way to put it.

I listened to her tell me about myself. She was condescending and cruel. I took it all on the chin. I'd seen this side of her before. Not with me. But things were different now. Saying sorry felt unoriginal and obvious. So, I didn't. Even though I was. She said a lot the last night I saw her. Starting with the Oxford English Dictionary definition of infidelity. Ending with a confession that she never liked any of the "rap shit" Bexx and I were addicted to, including Jay-Z.

That stayed with me. Having minor infidelities at this age was to be expected. To fabricate a love for Hov? The audacity. This bitch had some nerve. Sure, I wasn't completely oblivious to the fact that she'd rather listen to Beck or Bjork over a Just Blaze beat, but damn. She sure could fake it. An art form many of us have mastered. Most of us can fake an orgasm before we learn to drive. I zoned off. A product of my own neurosis. Wondering what else she faked. She was looking to push a button. It worked. Being uninterested in Kanye is one thing. To blatantly disrespect the living rap God that is Jay-Z? Treasonous. There's no coming back from that.

Look, I hated hurting her. I hated myself more for hurting her. I wanted to explain that I misinterpreted our last conversation about exclusivity. Three weeks prior, she went on and on about how her experience with women eclipses mine. Blatantly stating that if I still feel attracted to men and want to act on it, she understands. Maybe I took that and ran with it. Awarding myself a probationary period to wean off dick like antibiotics. I said none of that. I always hated explained intentions. Figured, if someone is meant to get me, they'll get me. I never took to shoving my disposition down someone's throat.

There's no dignity in what I did. She was my escape. Loud and brash but beautiful, and she knew it. Making the combination that much more obnoxious. She knew that, too, but didn't give a shit. She was right not to forgive me. I had no plan of cutting things off with the guy at the gym. Somewhere in my sick head, I thought I could convince both of them to let me date them both. Probably too much Real Sex HBO before bed.

I knew Lolita was finished with me. And I, her. I dated the gym guy for a few years after we split. Slumming it back in the north Valley. I thought we were in love because we'd cum at the same time. He ran some basketball league and was nice enough. But too vanilla to keep, even though he was black. More importantly, he was no her.

White Men Can't Jump

"I've never loved the wrong person, but I have loved the right people at the wrong time. The wrong life. The wrong moment." -- Dominic Riccitello

They say you get three great loves in your life. The first often happens at a young age. You eventually grow apart or call it quits over trivial shit. When you get older, you'll look back on it as "diluted love." But the truth is, it was love for what you knew love to be at the time. You get out of that relationship without suffering much collateral damage. A couple of bumps and bruises. A flesh wound, at worst. Nothing you can't handle.

The second love is hard. You get hurt in this one. Fetal position in the shower hurt. It's a love that teaches lessons and forces strength out of you. By any fucking means necessary. This love includes agonizing pain, lies, betrayal, drama, and baggage far too bulky to fit in the overhead compartment. It provides the perfect landscape to figure out what you love and hate about love. I'd call it a trainwreck, but shit, even train wrecks are worth watching. It teaches you to be closed off, careful, and cautious. This love leaves little room for happiness. None of that happy-go-lucky or misery loves company bullshit. This misery loves loneliness. The fewer witnesses to your misery, the better.

On a scale from Slim Shady to Malibu's Most Wanted, Brock clocked in at about an even seven. He wasn't a rapper, although his wardrobe begged to differ. You know that token white guy that only hangs out with black people, exclusively fucks women with melanin, and worships the Jordan One silhouette like it's God? Well, I dated him for like half a decade. Give or take. He's a transplant from Santa Barbara. One of those relationships that it's all said and done you think, shit, I should've kept him in the fucking friend zone. The worst feeling in the world is heartbreak with a side of I didn't want to date him in the first place. That's the kind of truth that stings when you swallow.

    If you completely ignore the undying loyalty to conservativism, Santa Barbara wasn't such a shit place to disappear to. Just an hour up the coast. You don't even have to get off the 101 freeway. I went once with my girl scout troop to check out the Santa Barbara Mission. To be honest, I can't remember a damn detail from that day, other than sitting by my mom on a train. My second time was with Raychel and Ashlee during senior year. We were hopped up on a blow rampage, running up and down State Street in half-naked Halloween costumes with what seemed like Southern California's entire teenage population. The drugs didn't even intensify our creativity. We trampled through the streets dressed as a sexy nurse, a stripper cop, and a slutty army brat. About as basic as we wanted to be.

    The Santa Barbara I knew with Brock was different than the one I'd been introduced to before. It was slow and romantic. We'd eat Lobster on the beach, and smoke ourselves silly in the hotel room. He'd show me private beaches and secret "locals only" scenic views. We were sweet in Santa Barbara. Shit was different there. It was the place that convinced me that we could be more than friends. And I've never been an easy audience to convince. So, after months of reluctance, I threw in the towel.

After one of our regular visits to the republican infested oasis, I came back to L.A. with a whole entire boyfriend. I hadn't been in a relationship in a while, which wasn't unintentional. Delusionally, I waited for an uproar of unwarranted opinions surrounding my new dating status. I was at the age where you think people give a shit what you do. As a teenager, I had the audacity to care what other people thought. In my twenties, I stopped caring about other people's opinions. In my thirties, I realized no one gives a fuck either way. There was the occasional elderly black man that usually resembled Morgan Freeman shaking his head in disappointment when we'd walk past him hand in hand, but other and that, everyone seemed to be happy that we were happy. And for a while we were. Brock was my best friend. We had everything in common, even the stuff we hated.

After dating for six months, we moved in together, for no other reason besides being uncontrollably addicted to each other, and having no other choice. You couldn't tell where one of us stopped and the other began. Everything that once made me cringe suddenly felt natural with him. PDA, romance, vulnerability, all that other mushy shit. It takes a real man to turn a cynic into a hopeless romantic, but he did. We'd listen to our favorite songs, driving through the city, making new memories in our old favorite places. He thawed my cold little sarcastic heart out like he had a defrost setting.

I was madly in love with my best friend. This is the shit fairy tales are made out of, I thought. Not that I ever subscribed to that Disney Princess bullshit. My dad never let us watch Disney movies growing up, for one reason and one reason only. Walt Disney was a fuckin fascist. After doing my own research, I found my dad's accusations to be a little off. At the risk of tarnishing the happily ever after facade, Walt was technically nazi affiliated, a flagrant racist, and a sexist that enthusiastically embraced anti-Semites. Nevertheless, I was in the kind of love where you would think I was rescued from some medieval tower. He was my person...until he wasn't. And when he wasn't, shit hit the fan.

Maybe it was me. Maybe my emotions turned me into an emotional psychopath. On a regular afternoon like any other, he was packing for a work trip and I was drinking tea on the couch. It was after one of those long, excruciating nights that I would fall asleep on the couch because conforming my body to an "L" shaped sofa was easier than lying next to him. You awaken with a lump in your throat and a knot in your back. And even that feels better than struggling through a conversation with someone who doesn't want to have it. Someone whose love used to make me love myself more. More than I did right now. More than I was about to in the next moments to come. I've never been one of those women that can bite my tongue. One of those people that can sit with an elephant in the room without letting a single word slip through their lips. I was still infected with an immaturity that would find a way to show me who's boss. He continued to go about packing. Walking from one room to the next looking for essentials. Phone charger, shoes, weed, hoodies, laptop etc.

"Are you seriously not going to say anything to me?" I didn't know what to say. Burden shifting felt like the opportune way to go.

"What do you want me to say, Brenn?" I could tell he was defeated in his eyes. He had been for a while. I knew that I did that to him. I just didn't know how to fix it anymore.

"I don't know. Something. Anything." I didn't feel like I was asking for too much. Just basic communication. What is it about men where they all have the emotional intelligence of a toddler when it comes to effectively communicate? Maybe that was the catch. Maybe I was no longer that woman. Maybe we killed the love and stuck around so long that we could smell it decay. It smelled like shit.

"I don't have anything to say," he said.

"So, you come home wasted after your phone died, AGAIN. And you mysteriously had no car charger, AGAIN? Don't say a word to me, AGAIN? Pass out, wake up to go back to New York, and you have nothing to say before you leave?" I hated sounding like a condescending sportscaster calling plays, but if he was going to play stupid, then I was going to write that shit down in crayon so he could understand it.

"WHAT THE FUCK DO YOU WANT ME TO SAY, BRENN?!" He slammed his carry-on down on the coffee table in frustration. The coffee cup of English breakfast with three raw sugars and some cream stirred in flew up into the air and landed all over me.

"ARE YOU FUCKING KIDDING ME!?" I responded.

He stood there silent. I knew he wanted to say it was an accident. That he didn't mean to, but he didn't. Round two: ding! The gloves were off. I don't know if it was the four years of resentment or the hatred I'd built up for him the past year for letting something so special turn to shit, but I was all over that motherfucker like a bad rash. Swinging my fists, like he was Monique in the parking lot and I was sixteen again. Talking shit with every hit like a pissed off parent.
"GET...THE...FUCK...OUTTA...HERE...WITH...THAT...BITCH ASS...SHIT...NIGGA! YOU GOT ME ALL THE WAY FUCKED UP!" You know how bilingual Spanish chicks, start speaking Spanish when they're pissed off or fucking? Well, I'm not sure why, but when I'm pissed off I turn into Remy Ma. Or someone like her.

He did what all good men do when their crazy girlfriend physically attacks them. He bobbed, weaved, and restricted me as much as possible. Like Jay-Z did Solange in the elevator. He pressed turbo on his packing and got the fuck out of there once I tired myself out. Leaving me alone with my anger. It was the first time I understood exactly why Left-Eye did what she did. Not that I had it in me to burn the house down. If burning your man's house down were the big leagues, I was still playing in pop warner. I went into the guest room that slowly transitioned into a shrine for all his sneakers, and poured red Gatorade all over his favorite pairs. If I was going to fuck this up then I was going to do it 'till the very last drop.

Surprisingly, we stayed together after that. Miserably together, but still together. Maybe there were split seconds of possibility, but if there were, I can't remember them. They must have been few and far between. I'd love to tell you that some seductive vixen came between us and tore our happy home apart. It would definitely make for a better story. The truth is a lot more mundane. We destroyed our relationship all by ourselves. No supporting cast or features. He turned into some refurbished version of himself. A workaholic that would get wasted and pass out in bathtubs at hotel parties. As for me? I could hardly recognize myself anymore. I'd sleep through the day, wishing to have a different life, smoking myself numb to all the emotions that were paralyzing me. We would pass each other without saying a word like ships in the night, at home—long surpassing the place where we could simply talk it out. We were different books that were written in different languages, that sit on different shelves, in different sections of forgotten libraries.

Fighting about everything from personal politics to social media. For two months I walked around with a burka around my face and told him, he didn't deserve to look at me because every picture he posted of me was hideous. I told him he was trying to trick our friends into thinking I'm uglier than I am. On a scale from one to Kanye, I was bat shit crazy. So about an even eight. That creepy thing about crazy is that once it took over my psyche, I couldn't see past it.

The frustration surrounding the reality that I couldn't find my footing creatively didn't help. He was depressed at the idea of too many opportunities coming his way. To be fair, music and fashion aren't the most easygoing industries, but execs in both were on his dick. And there I was with my thumb up my ass wishing for a sliver of what he had. When we weren't fighting, we were arguing, and when we weren't arguing, we were bickering. Everything was something. Small shit turned into big shit. Big shit was catastrophic.

I didn't realize it at the time, but cultural differences also began to weigh on me. It became painfully clear that my only actual experience in dating white boys was all the way back in eighth grade. There was my first kiss, Ryan Ellison, the local private school skater that resembled Devon Sawa and still probably holds the crown for my healthiest relationship to date, and then, my two-week relationship with Tyler Wilder voted Best All-Around. Whatever that means. We broke up when I missed his bar mitzvah to go to the Hard Knock Life Concert. My only excuse was that Hov would only be in town a few nights, but since he's turning into a man, he'll be a man for the rest of his life. It didn't go over as well as it did when I was rehearsing it in my bathroom mirror. If I had to rate myself in the white boy dating department, I'd probably give myself two stars. Would not recommend. Played in the minors. Never went pro.

Have you ever dated a white guy whose parents got divorced when they were young? It's the single most traumatic thing they've dealt with and trust me, you're going to hear about it. Between that and the never-ending complaints about how success was draining the joy out of him, I could recite both pity party monologues by memory. Beyond that, I'd never heard of being mentally drained by too much opportunity. I was praying that one of the seeds I'd planted over the last few years would sprout, and here he was drowning in offers and reacting like he was being waterboarded. That was when nearly every inch of adoration that I once had for him flew out the window. I couldn't wrap my head around it.

The guy I dated before him, saw his mother murdered in front of his eyes. My boyfriend, before that, was under the impression that his dad was dead. Later learning, at twenty-three, that wasn't the case. Even my ex-girlfriend had been through more shit than him. A couple of six-figure contracts suddenly turned him into this "poor me" prostitute, and I wanted no parts.

I stuck around for a couple more years. I've always been a sucker for self-destruction. I guess the truth is that I hoped the lobster loving lover boy would rear his shaved head again and remind me why I loved him in the first place. Unbeknownst to me, that motherfucker had left the building long ago. The end result? I wasted my pretty years on a "glorified blackspert." You know the ones, those appointed white dudes that work in black music to advise other older out of touch white dinosaurs on black culture.

*[**Blackspert - noun** / ˈblak ˌspərt/ a melanin deficient person who has a comprehensive and authoritative knowledge of or skill in black culture.]*

The demise of us can only be compared to dying with my eyes open. I wanted him to end it. I waited for him to end it. I prayed that he would end it. Despite my dying hopes and dreams, he didn't. He let the misery linger above us for as long as physically possible. I began to mourn the relationship while I was still in it. A trait my ex always said I mastered at a young age. A cheap apartment in New York became the object of his attention. The cute little traditional Toluca Lake duplex we once agreed on was going to soon be in my rearview, as would he. Every broken promise and half-truth was about to be as long gone as ten years ago. I hated that I had to be the one to pull the trigger.

He had an extended work trip. Standard. It was meant to be for two weeks. That rolled into four weeks, a trip to Vegas, a trip to the Hamptons, back to Vegas, one "I left my phone in a cab" one "I got stung by a jellyfish and went to the hospital," and a slew of other excuses. He was always partial to the kind of lies that would insult your intelligence. He'd been gone for a little over a month. Exactly the amount of time that I needed to source a little studio apartment in Sherman Oaks for one. The day he landed, he came home to my brother, cousin, dad, and a moving truck. It didn't require much reading between the lines. We talked ourselves stupid over the past few years. There was nothing left to say, besides, "The truck has to be back by six."

He slept over the first night in my new studio. The mattress was on the floor. About an inch higher than any hope I had for us. We pretended nothing was wrong. Like we couldn't hear the sound of us breaking. We walked to get pancakes in the morning. I cried into my mimosa. A smooth combination of cavalier cruelty and fabricated compassion with the artificial flavoring of maple syrup sat across from me. The last meal we ever shared. I hated him for weeks after that. Okay, months. Fine, fuck it, it's been years.

    We shared a few tequilas and made some dumb decisions at the top of 2017. He moved to Manhattan Beach with a producer he managed. I guess New York was done with him. My once soulmate was now a stringy-haired surfer, doing his very best Big Lebowski impression on a daily basis. Not even his echo sounded familiar. But I was on the rebound from my most recent situationship, and he felt safe. We spoke about things we couldn't before now that the emotion had run its course. Both taking accountability and laughing at our shortcomings. He even confessed to being a fuckin' coward. Well, not exactly. His words were that he never would've been the one to end it because he loved me too much. I appreciated the honesty even though it was technically bullshit. He'd tuck his grown out saltwater drenched hair behind his ear every time he lied. It was nothing new.

    He plays golf and surfs all day now when he isn't working. I always thought golf was condescending. It screams I have enough time to waste fifteen hours throwing back beers and chasing a ping-pong size ball around all day, and you have to deal with the real world. He said he bought a house somewhere in Benedict Canyon. We catch up on life from time to time. Usually, to discuss a mutual friend who passed away. It's come to that. The first time, it was a tattoo artist we both used. Nice guy with a fixation for mood stabilizers and muscle relaxers. I've got a dainty little victorian key he drew that decorates my left wrist. Drug addiction and depression are still undefeated. Hate it had to be you, Norm.

More recently, it was a writer we both knew. One of those strong black women that inspire other strong black women. I know because I'm one of them. She wrote books and films and shows. A rap nerd by nature and a writer at heart. She was everything I wanted to be, and I never even got the chance to tell her. The type of woman whose brilliance even Brock couldn't ignore. She seemed so certain and intentional. We talked before the details came out about her suicide, which only poured salt in the wound of her departure. We'd say everything you would expect.

"How could this happen?"

"Why did this happen?"

"I had no idea." A general symphony of shock and sorrow.

This place can be so damn unforgiving. After wearing out condolences, we'd shoot casualties back and forth until winding up on the dating topic. Who he's seeing, who I'm seeing, how it's going if it's going. Naturally, we grew out of commonalities a lifetime ago, and dating was the least common denominator. Customarily the conversation came with a fair amount of judgment. That's the thing about exes. We're all victims of our own perspective, and although that's subject to change, with your ex, it doesn't budge. He's the same asshole I left, and I'm that bitch he grew to hate. When it's over, you hang on to the bad just as much as you hung on to the good before it ended.

Still entertaining each other's uncertainties. I'd pretend to care about his trysts with "it" girls or pop stars or stylists or influencers. And I would inquire about behavioral patterns I'm trying to recognize in myself.

As much as it pained me to admit it, he was still fucking hilarious. Continuing to hold the title for the most significant connection I'd ever made. I always found myself fishing for his opinion. Still. Even though I completely disregarded our relationship as a tragically long case of imposter syndrome. The cut and dry version is that I told him who and what I wanted, often and early. He then did what he could to fit into that mold for as long as he could until he couldn't take it anymore. Neither could I, I guess. Maybe I was doing it too. I didn't see him when I looked at him anymore. I saw through him, and the sight sickened me. And I wouldn't be surprised if he said the same damn thing.

When anyone has gone through enough life to get over their ego, you realize that relationships fall apart all the time. Not because of him, or because of me but because of timing. Because I couldn't be the woman I am to my man when I knew him, and because he couldn't be the man he'll be to whoever he ends up with when he knew me. It doesn't make us wrong for trying. Maybe naive, but not wrong. Most women play a game in their heads with their ex called Whoever Finds Happiness First Wins. As far as Brock and I go, I'm gone, and he's still there. I guess we can call it even. There are no saints or virgins here. This city fucks everyone.

Part Two - The City

Only In L.A.

> *"Los Angeles, where everyone's so actively working on cheerfulness and mental and physical health that if they sense you're down, they shun you."* --Mindy Kaling

Only in L.A. are dogs pushed in strollers and kids walked on leashes.

Only in L.A. would Beverly Hills High have an oil field on campus.

Only L.A. would make up twenty percent of the nation's homeless population while dishing out $1.8 billion to the LAPD.

Only in L.A. would The County Morgue have a gift shop.

Only in L.A. would someone anonymously commit suicide by jumping off the Hollywood sign.

Only in L.A. would someone ask if your teeth are natural.

Only in L.A. will you see a firework show while the hills are on fire.

Only in L.A. would you hear someone taking legal advice from a Barista.

Only in L.A. are dog chiropractors and energy healers respectable professions.

Only in L.A. will perfectly adequate drivers turn into student drivers at the first drop of rain.

Only in L.A. can you simultaneously party with a porn star and a politician.

Only in L.A. will you see Jay Leno driving a different hot rod every day on your commute to work.

Only in L.A. do you get 80-degree weather in December.

Only in L.A. will you see a pit bull in a cardigan at the dog park.

Only in L.A. is goat yoga a thing.

Only in L.A. does rain catch us off guard every season since.

Only in L.A. is cry therapy a form of self-love.

Only in L.A. would there be a massage parlor specifically to get your face massaged.

Only in L.A. would you go to the Hollywood Forever cemetery for movie night.

Only in L.A. will you see someone with no house and no food bumping oldies on the boulevard through a big ass Blue Tooth Speaker.

Only in L.A. would pranksters change the Hollywood sign to Hollyweed on 420.

Only in L.A. does "I've had no work done" mean you've gotten a tit-job and some botox. The starter pack.

Only in L.A. will you catch a suspect trying to breakdance away from an arrest after a high-speed chase.

Only in L.A. will seeing the Back To The Future car in traffic calm your anxiety.

Only in L.A. is "damn, no invite," the most annoying phrase known to the human language.

Only in L.A. can you go to the beach and see the snow on the same day.

Only in L.A. do people believe in a thing called "Earthquake weather."

Only in L.A. can you see a girl out with a guy who looks old enough to be her dad and not bat an eye because rent is due, and you can't pay bills with sunshine.

Only in L.A. would you know that when you're asked if you listen to hip-hop by anyone with headphones, the answer is always no.

Only in L.A. would fans camp out overnight for a yard sale at Chris Brown's house.

Only in L.A. do men think rented luxury cars make their dick bigger.

Only in L.A. is traffic a standard form of measurement.

Only in L.A. do you get approached to be on a reality show while pretending to hike.

Only in L.A. do you see teenage kids driving Bentleys and adults catching the bus.

Only in L.A. would IHOP offer valet parking.

Only in L.A. would there be a security-guarded mural on a vacant wall made "for influencers" only.

Only in L.A. do you have to suffer through your uber driver's mix-tape.

Only in L.A. is marrying a rich dude a popular career path.

Laurel Canyon

> *"Ask anyone in America where the craziest people live, and they'll tell you California. Ask anyone in California where the craziest people live, and they'll say, Los Angeles. Ask anyone in Los Angeles where the craziest people live, and they'll tell you Hollywood. Ask anyone in Hollywood where the craziest people live, and they'll say Laurel Canyon. And ask anyone in Laurel Canyon where the craziest people live, and they'll say Lookout Mountain. So I bought a house on Lookout Mountain."*
> *-- Joni Mitchell*

If the Canyon was good enough for certified sex symbols and rumored lovers, James Dean and Marlon Brando, it was good enough for my folks. I find comfort in knowing that two of the biggest heartthrobs in Hollywood history were more interested in their secret sadomasochistic relationship than they were their female Hollywood counterparts or fanbase, but that's just the way my sick sense of humor works. This place has a way about it. Even if you cut out all the legendary shit that's happened in these hills, it's still one of my favorite places in the world.

In the 70's granola-infused hippie collectives, folk musicians, and psychedelic rockers, took to the place like flies on shit. Twisted roads, hidden cottages with stained-glass windows, and the fresh smell of wild eucalyptus made an idyllic backdrop for aspiring musicians to take drugs, form bands, break up, and form new bands. Making Laurel Canyon the nucleus of counter-culture and rock star fucking central.

It's where Jim Morrison wrote "Love Street" when he lived behind the Canyon Country Store. And where Joni Mitchell wrote "Ladies Of The Canyons." Jackson Browne lived in a basement beneath Glenn Frey. Still snuggled in the idyllic oasis, convincing enough to fool you into thinking you're a world away from Los Angeles. That's the magic of the Canyon. The punch line of it all is that you could hit the Sunset Strip if you throw a rock hard enough. It was only five minutes away. Not that anyone gave a shit. Everyone was either stoned, fucking, writing, singing, recording, jamming, or rehearsing. And if they weren't doing that, they were still somewhere stoned and fucking.

People like Jimi Hendrix, Ringo Starr, and Eric Clapton would hang out at Mama Cas's house. The safe-haven for artistic luminaries. The neighborhood was infested with bohemia, and anyone craving a little edge or individualism clung to it like it was a life preserver for their creativity.

Around this time, less famous with absolutely no affiliation to any of these people, a sweet little couple lived at the end of Honey Drive. An interracial couple, not that that's worth mentioning. She was a Spanish Hippie from a tiny statutory town in Colorado. Where the population was eight hundred something and the median income for a household was less than $20,000. Her name was Cheryl Montano. The oldest of four. She was beautiful with olive-toned skin and long black hair, with enough hippie garb to throw her in the "free love" category. She drove an old Volkswagen and worked at a bank. It was there that she met the love of her life, and fuck was he different than anyone she'd ever been with back in Colorado.

Derek was a radical investment banker, and Cheryl had just found out there was such a thing. Often the smartest, most charismatic man in the room. Just ask him. His confidence was a problem, but she liked challenges. She already moved from Alamosa to New York and back again, and now finally to L.A.

When enough time has gone by, people always say, "it was a simpler time," when referring to the past, but that's a load of shit if I ever heard it. The country was fresh off the VietNam War, and everyone was screaming to prove they still existed. Derek made it out of the Navy alive, embraced his passion for absolute radicalism, joined the black panthers, and fell in love with Cheryl. The rest was just noise.

They moved to Laurel Canyon from Cochran and Pico. And to this day, they describe that small crevice of time in the early '70s, in that Canyon, as the best years of their life. They say it was like that monotone sitcom with Ted Danson. A place "where everybody knows your name." A lot was going on in those hills, but they didn't give a shit who their neighbors were. Or even seem to notice.

They were wrapped up in each other. He got the girl, made it out the hood and the war with his mind intact, along with a promising career in finance, which is a lot more than most black men could say at the time. Growing up in the hood has a tendency of making a monster out of you. You witness too much, too young, and the time you'd need to process that caliber of trauma doesn't exist because there's something equally horrendous around the corner. It's designed that way, and not by accident. It's called systemic engineering, but that's another rant for another time, and we all have google.

That was then. Derek found a way out, and despite the undiagnosed PTSD, lucked-up on a slice of heaven in Cheryl. The quaint little duplex nestled in the Canyon, at the end of Honey Drive, was their haven. All the streets had some over-romanticized woodsy name that sounds like it came straight out of Pleasantville, USA. But damn, it felt good. More than that, it was cheap, and there was something contagiously poetic about it.

If you would've told Derek then that he'd be teaching his daughter how to drive the back streets of that very Canyon one day, he'd probably say nothing with a smirk. A calculated son of a bitch, he had his life planned since he got here. Every fucking detail. I rode in the backseat of the tangled streets in Laurel Canyon, listening to music that some of its residents created there without even knowing it. Now I've driven those roads so much, I can do it with a blindfold, in the rain. Not that I recommend it.

Significant gentrification came through the Canyon like a bat out of hell by the time I was born. Once I was "of age" or whatever they call it, I got ridiculously high and went on one of those tacky celebrity home tours, and all they pointed out was the Houdini Mansion and the massive residence where Brittany Murphy died. I spent most of my twenties completely asleep to the magic that sits in these hills. To the creative history that haunts the Canyon. Maybe I needed to be at an age where I could truly appreciate it before knowing all the juicy details. From the "Lost Nights" that John Lennon had to the Wonderland Murders. Also known as the Four on the Floor Murders, but my favorite story to come out of the Canyon is my parent's love story.

Embarrassingly, my time in the Canyon was spent being pretentious with the rest of the herd. Mount Olympus parties with models? hopped up on blow. Award show after-parties where grown men feed their insecurities by preying on young girls. Endless screenings, listenings, launches, releases, birthdays, barbeques, pool parties, and any excuse to show off a well-manicured backyard. The most frequent and predictable events are often brought to us in some mega-mansion at the top of the hill, rented out by some multi-million dollar brand collaborating with somebody who's anybody to sponsor a party. It sounds desperate, but it usually makes for a pretty good time: open bar, photo booths, gift bags. A private performance from some fill in the blank artist. Whoever's hot at the moment, and all that basic shit, we're all used to.

We're all vampires in the hills. Thirsty for sin. Hungry for pleasure. Carrying on to the next event like programmed robots. Brainwashed by the moment and held hostage by our vices. I was once told that I live a life of privilege and that I should have more respect for the lifestyle I've been afforded. While the first part is true, the second still makes me piss my pants laughing. To pretend that any of us are more or less than victims of circumstance is comical. I'm sure from the outside looking in, it's all glamour and glitz, with a side of heavy FOMO, but these pretentious parties are packed with vain and vapid souls, staring at screens waiting for their brains to turn on. It's all devastatingly predictable. No element of surprise. The idea of mystery is a long lost concept. Somehow none of that distracts from the fact that it all looks like so much fun.

What they don't tell you is that the painfully attractive model that seems a million times more beautiful in person held her fingertips under the cold running faucet before shoving them down her throat. Forcing herself to puke up the hors d'oeuvres she choked down at the party, feels to her, how cumming feels to most. They also don't talk about the fact that the hype beast baller got held at gunpoint for all that expensive gawdy shit he flashes on Instagram two days after the party. They skip mentioning Young What's His Name and Lil Whoever have a fundamental addiction to pills and sex. And leave out that your "couples goal" is the epitome of dysfunction. The guy cheats on his "woman crush Wednesday" nearly every damn day. It started when she would voluntarily participate in threesomes to please him. The poor broad didn't have a bicurious bone in her body, but he had money, which was understood to be a verbal agreement. Now he fucks whoever whenever depending on which way the wind blows. She grins and bears it because when she brings it up, shit gets aggressive. They leave all of that out in the movies and the songs.

They leave out that the guy all the girls have been masturbating to has an anonymous gay dating profile with no plans of ever coming out of the closet. They fail to mention that the liquor companies send free bottles to fill the bar, throw their logo on the step and repeat, and in return, get hundreds of baseless talent strung out on popularity promoting their product. The clothes you drool over are "gifted," which is code for when the person wearing them provides more value than if the brand sold the item. This happens with just about everything, from clothes to surgery to jewelry. Everything's transactional; name your price. They don't tell you about the trauma or terror or depression that this smoke and mirrors lifestyle can plant in someone. They leave out all the bits that can't be dressed up and sucked in. It's backward and elementary. The popular crowd rules the lunchroom, and if they like you, you're in. You benefit from the free shit too. The beauty products and trendy clothes and important invitations. You become one of these consumer addicted fembots without even realizing it. And as soon as you recognize the entitlement washing over you, it's too late to do a damn thing about it. Because now you don't just want it. You require it, and that's worse.

One night I took Laurel Canyon south, away from the valley, into the hills, where the Canyon crests over the top at Mulholland. I took that route to get to my office, but this time, I just wanted to hear an album in the car and go for a drive. That week was specifically stressful, and once I cleared Mulholland, it began raining. I cracked the window to smell the freshness and turned the volume up. All at once, everything was okay. There's something spiritual about driving Laurel Canyon to the sound of your favorite songs. Sometimes you'll catch a picturesque sunset. Or maybe get caught in the first rainfall. No matter the weather, it did something to you. It fixes you. It reminds you that you're not as great as they say or shit as they presume.

Maybe it's in my head. Maybe it's the history that tricks me into looking deeper than I should be. Maybe it's that if my parents didn't have that time in Laurel Canyon, my half-breed ass wouldn't be around to tell you about it.

IT ONLY SEEMS RANDOM

405 South

"In just a couple more days they're going to close the freeway, and you won't be able to go anywhere on the 405. As opposed to when it's open and you can't go anywhere on the 405."
--- Jay Leno

The 405 freeway is the epicenter of frustration. It also happened to be the connecting freeway for me to get home, most of my life. My parents got their shit together and bought a house in Porter Ranch when I was twelve—nestled at the end of a cul-de-sac in the windy serviceless little town that sits in the hills above the 118 freeway.

Now, when you're a middle-class suburban mixed chick perpetually overcompensating for the lack of exposure you had to black culture, you tend to be predictably attracted to niggas from the hood. On the flip side of that coin, when you're a nigga from the hood, that grew up idolizing rappers that oversaturated their music videos with exotic snobby light skin girls, you tend to be attracted to the "new valley girl" archetype.

Just for clarity, the original valley girl is essentially seen as a Cher Horowitz or Kelly Kapowsky. You know the type. Today, the valley has become infested with bi and tri-racial families, and the result is a sea of ethnically ambiguous kids overpopulating the 818, and I'm here for it.

*[**Valley -girl:** /ˈvalē/ɡərl/noun/ A socio-economic stereotype depicting a class of women characterized by the colloquial California English dialect Valleyspeak and materialism.]*

[New valley-girl: /n(y)oō/ ˈvalē/ɡɚrl/noun/ A new dimensionality to the stereotypical socioeconomic norm depicting a new wave of women, multicultural and multi-dynamic, they speak with a certain rhythm in their dialect and are inevitably attractive mixed females addicted to retail.]

Back to the story. If you take the 405 for long enough and hop on a connector, you'll end up in Compton, California. Compton is a peculiar place. Not for any of the reasons that Kendrick Lamar cited in Good Kid Maad City or any other predictable reasons. But more so, because it was exactly the opposite of what I expected. No one asked me what set I'm from. I didn't witness any black on black violence. I saw a community that gave a shit about their homes and the people in them. There were manicured lawns, ice cream trucks ringing through the streets while kids played outside in the community. Granted, I didn't spend much time in Compton. I can probably count how many times I've been there on both my hands; this is just how I saw it.

Like any other sheltered valley girl, I was drawn to Compton by a guy.

Case and point: Nieman was black and Japanese, hilarious, really easy to be around, and we got on like a house on fire. We were teenagers, and it's only fair that I now point out that he is currently a married man with an incredibly beautiful wife and equally impressive daughters. Not that any of that has anything to do with this story.

Nieman was best friends with Eric, who I'd known from our shameless pursuits in the music industry. Although, that journey ended a lot more tragically for me than it did him. I was fresh out of high school, and I was regularly accompanying the two of them on their Compton and Lynwood paper route. We'd hang out all night until four in the morning when they had to load up their Honda Accord with more newspapers than I'd ever seen at one time. I'd usually fall asleep on a pile of them in the back seat while the boys passed them out from house to house. Why did I do this? I still don't know, but I bring it up every time I see either of them just to remind them that I'm not bougie. A complex I've been fighting due to my dumb Valley accent for as long as I could speak. They were fun, and despite their current position as paperboys, they had dreams of Eric becoming a force in the industry as an artist and songwriter and Nieman finding success as his manager. Which they eventually did. Again, another story for another time.

One night, in particular, the three of us arranged to go bowling with my friend Shawna. Unbeknownst to her. Shawna was an aspiring model that fell into a girl group with yours truly. We spent a massive amount of time together in high school. Rehearsing, recording, performing, label meetings, management meetings, sleeping over at each other's houses in between, staying up all night writing songs, stressing out together when it was time to shop our demo. Yes, it was back when shopping your demo was an actual thing. Shawna had become less of a group member and more of a sister. She was unlike anyone I'd known. She knew about things that made me feel like a tasteless twat, like which high-end fashion designers to wear and when. She knew tons of people that seemed more important than me at the time, so when she was less than reluctant to tag along to go bowling in Compton, I couldn't pretend like it wasn't expected. Driving over an hour to go bowling was hardly an enticing offer in her eyes. Both bowling and Compton were individually repulsive adventures. And I had the audacity to invite her to do both. Unfortunately for her, I can be pretty persuasive when I want to be. I pulled the always classic and rarely overruled "take it for the team" card, which is an unwritten law in girl code that states that if one friend is interested in a guy, then you must accompany her while entertaining said guy's friend for the mere fact that it's what friends do. Not for nothing, it worked. I convinced her to come. We were six outfit changes and three attempts at applying winged eyeliner away from a night out in Compton. Disguised as a double date where I get to hang out with my current crush. Shit was looking up from where I was sitting.

    This was a time when getting ready required more than watching a youtube tutorial or saving a couple of outfits of the day to replicate "a look." And we have the flat iron burns, trucker hats, and airbrushed tank tops to prove it. At around eight o'clock, Nieman and Eric picked us up from my parents' house. Oh, the thrill of being overdressed and underage. We piled in the car. Nieman was driving; I was sitting in the passenger seat while Eric and Shawna were in the back. We were only on the road for about thirty minutes when Niems put the car in cruise control. I still don't know why. At that age, you drive faster than you need to at a failed attempt at impressing everyone else in the car. That said, we were cruising at about 85/90 mph when the steering wheel locked. Holy shit. I noticed Nieman struggling to regain control of the wheel.

Fuck. This was clearly going to get worse before it got worse, I thought.

We were in the carpool lane between the center divider and a semi-truck. As the freeway began to bend, we couldn't turn with it; the car was darting between the cement divider and tractor-trailer truck to the right. It was loud, like a gunshot or a firecracker, every time we made contact with one side or the other. You could hear the metal of the car grinding against the concrete. We ricocheted between it and the truck several times; sparks were flying. It felt chaotic, but we were silent, practically holding our breath before spinning out of control. None of us said a word. We were all scared shitless. There were a couple of other cars involved in the collision; all I was thinking was, this is how it ends. The car ultimately clipped a couple of cars in crossfire on our way to flipping off the 405 fucking freeway. Is this real life? It was, and we did. The car flipped all of four times and took us with it.

You could hear branches scraping the window and then complete darkness. I could smell smoke, but I couldn't see a thing.

"Is everyone okay?" I totally forgot Shawna was even in the back seat before I heard her voice.

"Uh-huh" was all I could get out.

"You good?" Nieman followed up.

"Yeah," Eric responded while taking off his seat belt.

We were all checking our bodies for injuries and taking a second to let the shock wear off.

"OMG, it's over. Fuck, that was insane," I said.

"Nothing's over, don't you smell that, this shit is gonna blow," Shawna said in a panic while opening her car door to run for her life. I tried to open my door, but it was lodged shut. I began hitting it with the back of my elbow. Probably some crap I saw in a movie.

The window didn't even crack before I realized I could hop in the backseat and exit through the same door Shawna did. The guys followed suit. I didn't realize how deep into the brush that the car had traveled after plunging off the 405 until it was time for us to climb through that brush to get back to civilization.

We crawled through an incline of dirt, mud, and bushes to make our way back to the side of the freeway. This wasn't the night I imagined, but you know what they say, God laughs while you're busy making plans. By the time we reached the shoulder of the road, Eric immediately ran in the opposite direction. Almost as if he was running away from us but towards the nearest right of way. In hindsight, I'm assuming he was pissed at Nieman for getting us into this shit, and that was his half-assed attempt at running it off. Or maybe dealing with the fact that we all had an actual real-life brush with death was a lot for one person to digest. The next thing I knew, he had his hands on his knees, hunched over while hyperventilating.

"You got your inhaler?" Nieman asked him. It was an incredibly inopportune time to learn that Eric is severely asthmatic. His breaths became more shallow, and you could hear the blockage from his lungs to his airway.

"In the car," he said while struggling to breathe.

"I'll go," I said before running down the hill back toward our car at emergency speed.

Or, at least, what I thought was emergency speed. I looked in the backseat and nothing. I looked under the seat and in the side compartments and—still, nothing. The car continued to smoke from the engine and was now making a high pitch noise that you'd think only a dog should be able to hear. I wasn't sure whether it was on its way to exploding or how much time I had before that happened. Frantically, I relocated my search to the front seat. I entered through the driver's side for the same reason I exited through the back seat earlier. I studied the center compartment like it was the PSAT's and still, nothing. I refused to go back up there without his inhaler. This is when the panic set in. I'm gonna die. He's gonna die. We're both gonna die. My parents are going to kill me.

I must speak to the fact that I've always believed that I was going to die young. I understand how stupid that sounds now that I'm an age that can hardly be considered "young," however youthful conspiracies can't be controlled. My baseless early death theory could be completely predicated on the fact that I watched way too many documentaries as a kid, and most of the subjects suffered unexpected deaths early on in life. Aaliyah, Left-Eye, Basquiat, Kurt Cobain. You get the point. It could be my ego, but I've always known I had something to say and assumed that no one would give a shit unless I kicked the bucket or Van Gogh'd myself.

The last place there was to look was the glove compartment. I opened it up and saw some registration papers and the corner of a silver circle. After shuffling the forms around, I could see it was, in fact, an inhaler. I shook it and heard a little click-clack and took my debatably heroic ass back up the hill. By the time I handed the inhaler to Eric, I was out of breath myself. He shook it up, placed the plastic actuator in his mouth, and pressed down while breathing in. He did it again. Shook it up and did it again.

"It's empty," he said as he gasped before adding,

"This is the wrong one."

As much as I love the idea of saving the day, a bitch can only take so much. I struggled to find a subtle way of letting him know that there was no way in hell; I was going back to the car. But all I could muster up at this point was some Sia lyrics

"just breathe," I told him with my hand on his back.

Sure, it was a cop-out, but, it was all he could do.

About half an hour later, the police showed up. Ready and willing to question us over our involvement in what now looked like a five-car pile-up. Including the eighteen-wheel truck and a partridge in a pear fuckin tree.

"If you're a part of this, then where is your car?" one of the officers asked us in a suspicious tone. We looked at him in confusion and said nothing. I've still yet to meet someone who would crawl through the dirt of the 405 to "pretend" they got in a five-car collision. But when you have more melanin than a little bit in L.A., you're always subjected to ridicule by law enforcement. This was nothing new for any of us. We all pointed in the direction of the car. None of us felt we had to dignify the unwarranted suspicion with a verbal response.

"Are you little motherfuckers out of your mind?" a short, wire-haired woman came speed walking in our direction. She was enraged over the bumper damage on her Volvo and needed us to know it.

"Look what you little shits did to my car." she continued. She was a dead ringer for one of those middle-aged women that look forward to soap opera conventions, so I have to imagine that bumper damage could be a lot more traumatic for her than it would the average person.

"Fuck your Volvo. We almost died." Shawna didn't seem to share in my sentiment.

She was pissed that the evil version of Molly Shannon was pissed, and she had a right to be. The officers calmed her down and continued questioning us when two fire engines pulled up. The fire department ended up having to cut down a tree to retrieve Nieman's car. They were shocked that we made it out alive, but we weren't. We had things to do and shit to prove. The rest of the night unfolded as expected. My parents picked us up, took us to the hospital to get checked out, and then lectured me for what seemed like months.

Don't get me wrong; I know plenty of people who have lived in L.A. their whole lives and haven't flipped off a freeway. I also know more people than I'm willing to admit that have experienced drunken, tragic, near-fatal, slow-motion, interstellar, apocalyptic, terrifyingly violent, and stupid car accidents. To say that it's more likely to happen in L.A. feels unfair, but when you take the increasing population into account, then add that to the number of cars on the road, and times that by the fact that everyone in L.A. drives 85% worse at night or on the rare occasion that it rains; It seems like a logical conclusion to jump to.

      Statistically, car crashes are the fourth most common cause of premature death in Los Angeles. The 405 happens to be among the top ten deadliest highway stretches in California. I've never lived anywhere that hasn't been the most fill in the blank in the world, so I wouldn't know the difference either way.

The Trouble With Cool

"It's pretty clear now that what looked like it might have been some kind of counterculture is, in reality, just the plain old chaos of undifferentiated weirdness." -- Jerry Garcia

The trouble with cool shit is that it's only cool until people find out about it. As soon as the general public knows, it instantly depreciates in cool value. I've been on the hunt for relatively unknown cool shit for as long as I can remember. Unsigned artists, unknown authors, hole in the wall restaurants, secret gardens, private beaches, they all have a designated space in my heart. It's probably why I consider Coachella or Art Basel to be like the Disneyland of music and art. When everybody knows about something special, it just doesn't feel special anymore.

Growing up, I longed for a party scene that no longer existed. Massive underground parties in abandoned warehouses. Ones where you'd get a mysterious blank envelope with a dissolvable capsule in it. Along with directions to dissolve it in water to reveal the password you state at the door. No password, no entrance. The soundproof doors would open to hundreds of people dancing to something ignorant and hard as fuck like Black Rob's Whoa! Followed by a Jay-Z set that everyone gets belligerent to until the sun comes up. I don't know; maybe I've seen too many movies.

It probably has something to do with watching my brother thrive as a jungle D.J. in the rave scene at thirteen. I once got one of his ex-girlfriends to take me with her to a dessert party he was spinning at. He was always off on some adventure in some dessert, warehouse, forest, or cave. Doing cool shit, I wasn't cool enough to do. Monica was the ex and didn't take much convincing. She was pretty cool. She looked like a pixie or a fairy with arms covered in multicolored plastic beaded bracelets and glitter smudged on the sides of her eyes. Her hair was short and blonde; but could just as easily be pink, turquoise, or violet, depending on her mood. She had the whole Drew Barrymore from Mad Love vibe fucking nailed. Most of the girls' Morgan brought around were candy ravers that worshiped him as the techno God he considered himself to be. They all had an aesthetic that screamed, I'm with the D.J., and I love happy hardcore. She was no different.

  In 1994, the government passed a law banning large events featuring music "characterized by the emission of a succession of repetitive beats." Raves were officially illegal. None of that stopped them from happening. The Caladan desert parties were a direct example. They were thrown by a group of dudes named Buddha, Doc, Peter Pan, and some other fictional names I can't remember. Their crew was called Storm Riders, after some martial arts flick I never heard of, and they all went to USC. Caladan Four was a little less than two hours away. Somewhere near Edwards Air Force Base. My brother firmly denied my request to come several times over the week leading up to it.

  Monica was an easier audience. They just broke up a few days before but stayed friendly because of PLUR. The understood philosophy that all rave heads live by Peace, Love, Unity, and Respect.

It was like an alternate universe. Everyone called Morgan "Lowtech" and called his friend Mark "Quiki". They had a party crew called Trip. Made up of a bunch of weirdos from the valley and Inland Empire. One guy thought he was a full-on cartoon tiger. Monica and her friend picked me up in her Camaro. We got gas and hit the road to the clandestine gathering. I vaguely remember getting in a car accident and having to ditch the Camaro by the side of the road. I figured the plan was fucked once the car tapped out on us. But all we did was hop on laps in a truck that was caravanning behind us and continued on.

When we pulled up to the anti-establishment all-nighter, it looked straight out of a scene from Fantasia. People were *glowsticking, glowstringing, gloving,* candy-walking, Drum and Bass Stepping, and everything in between. There were LED lights bouncing off the tenting—Red, yellow, green, blue. I took a sugar-free Redbull to the head and spent an unknowable amount of time dancing to trance and electronica. I must've forgotten where I was and how I got there because I was actually excited to see Morgan from a distance. I ran up to him. "What the fuck?" was all that came out of his mouth. "Monica brought me." I was too excited to realize that qualified me to be a snitch. "Of course she did. You were in the fucking Camaro?" Yikes. I didn't know that he heard about the Camaro hiccup. I stood there, silently attempting to give him puppy-dog eyes.

His pupils were dilated as big as marbles. Years later, he told me he was peaking on a classic party combination of MDMA and something else at the exact moment I ran up to him. Talk about a buzzkill. "I can't do this right now," he said before walking away. I didn't see him for the rest of the night. Until it was time to arrange my ride home, I also can't remember how I got home or who with. All things considered, I guess I got home safely. As much of a shit show that night turned out to be, I thoroughly enjoyed every second of it. I hadn't realized that it would instill an unrealistic party expectation in me. But it did.

By the time I was of age, partying consisted of gathering around overpriced alcohol in a bucket of ice like thirsty gazelles at a watering hole. It wasn't exactly what one would consider "fun." Standard club practice meant that you couldn't show up before midnight, or you were too eager. And you couldn't leave after one because only stragglers stay until the lights come on, and the club closes at two. Allotting precisely one hour to get your kicks while you're young enough to get them. The rules weren't discussed, just understood. Joey made sure of that. He was our designated socializing guru. If there was something to do or somewhere to be, he knew about it. Nine times out of ten, it was one of his events. He worked as a publicist and thank God. I don't think I could stomach his perspective on a lot of shit if he couldn't justify it with "it's my job." And he was good at it. He knew everyone, even the people you'd think weren't worth knowing—everybody's best friend, including mine.

I've known Joey since we were eighteen. Like all good friendships, when we met, we couldn't fucking stand each other. Our only saving grace was that he was close with my play sister, and I was close with his real sister.

[play·sister /noun /p ˈsistər/ A woman or girl of no relation to you that you are undoubtedly close to.]

He's the kind of friend you never wanted. A judgemental, shallow, self-absorbed, one-dimensional, delusionally confident, certified womanizer. Okay, that's not true. Women have never inspired a sexual thought in his cocky little head. He's as gay as Christmas. Manizer just doesn't have the same ring to it.

Sexual Prawless aside, Joey was known in the city for three things. Number one that he is constantly surrounded by a flock of beautiful women. It's been that way since high school. It works for everyone involved. Straight guys want to be around him so that he can hook them up with his girlfriends, and he wants to be around straight guys in hopes of playing just the tip to see where they fall on the sexuality spectrum. The second thing Joey is known for is getting to the bag. This power-top has worked with them all. He's booked, signed, launched, collaborated, and sponsored his way through this town, leaving no checks on the table. The sole thing with any ability to distract Joey from dick and celebrity culture was, is, and will continue to be money. Last but not least, his most monumental credit would have to be his reputation for throwing some of the most notorious and exclusive events the city has ever seen.

Last year at his ugly sweater party Puff Daddy got shit-faced while performing All of the Benjamins and fell off a coffee table. It's one of my most cherished Christmas memories.

That was after Meg the Stallion performed some Hot Girl shit while chugging D'usse on the couch, and Trey Songz and Meek Mill made every attending Instagram model's panties wet. Not bad for a house party. As I said, Joey can throw an event in his sleep.

With every year that passes by, socializing gets a more boring layer of sophistication thrown on top of it. It's like old fashion fun is struggling to get out in a pit of maturity and consequences that move like quicksand. The more you struggle to escape, the deeper you fall. We don't go out to drink ourselves stupid anymore. Or even to dance until we're sweaty. I dance sitting down now, and wild obscurities have turned into wine tastings. Or spa nights where you do basic shit in a group, like wash your face and pop your pimples.

I always thought I hated people until I was legally restricted from seeing them. As if being an adult isn't enough of a buzzkill, Covid-19 has turned existence into an episode of The Handmaid's Tale. The first few months were rough. Everyone panicked and bought up all the toilet paper. A million and a half reported cases later, people are finding creative ways to continue living. I've been to more birthday drive-by's and zoom parties than I ever intended. The official state of emergency lockdown started in March of last year. Rounding out ten consecutive months of rainy day schedule. Heads up seven up.

You can imagine my excitement when my boyfriend told me we'd be going out to dinner Sunday night. I would've gone to the opening of an envelope. I have been so bored I threw a bar mitzvah for his dog's birthday last week, and we aren't even Jewish. I asked all the expected questions. Will the tables be socially distanced? Is it inside? Are they going to check our temperatures? Do we have to test first? He answered none of them. He hated questions almost as much as I hated his hate for questions. "Babe, I already sent you everything; just check your phone." I did. The message read as follows:

Hello Secret Supper Club members! Thank you for joining us Sunday evening. Please note that your dinner start time is 8:30 pm sharp.

We want to take this time to give you the secret knock and password.

Once you knock, a doorkeeper will open the slot and ask for the password before you are let in.

Knock: 3 distinct knocks (knock....knock....knock)
Password: "Guinea Pig"

You will embark upon a 15-course tasting menu that will be cooked over an open fire right in front of you by our professional hospitality team. Chef Ventura will lead the culinary team along with Chef Sanchez and Chef Jack, and Chef Hotchkin. Mr. Goldberg will provide hospitality. The mixologist is Bradley Fry. Of course, your host will be Chef Sayegh.

Please be 10 minutes early! It is very important that you follow the timing of this event.

Car service is encouraged and will be provided—location to be disclosed twenty-four hours prior to the event. Upon arrival, look for the Jackrabbits Lair Logo and follow the pathway leading to two wooden gates. Once you knock on the gates, an associate will allow you thirty seconds to recite the secret password, and you'll be let in. After the meal, you will be able to enjoy the lounge with drinks and cannabis if you so choose.

We cannot wait to serve you!

Sunday night crept up on us rather quickly. I put the location in google maps as soon as they sent it to us. Zooming in on the exact address in Street View. It didn't look as Illuminati as one would think. In fact, it looked like some misplaced house taken out of Martha's Vineyard and plopped in the middle of L.A. When the car arrived, it was clear that my man hadn't read the invite. "We're here? Now what?" He had no clue what was going on. My excited to be out of the house ass, felt like I was in a game of clue on my way to crack the case. It was Colonel Mustard in the library with the wrench.

I recognized the jackrabbit logo from the invitation. "This way," I said, pointing. "Are you sure?" He wasn't the type to be easily convinced. "Yeah, that's the symbol, we have to go this way, knock three times and say guinea pig." He probably thought I was making it up. We followed the dark pathway. When we reached the gate, my boyfriend knocked three distinct strong knocks. Two eyes appeared in a slot, and we could faintly hear the mouth below the eyes mutter out "password." "Guinea pig," he said confidently. Guess he believed me after all. Both gates slowly opened, revealing a kitchen of chefs putting the finishing touches on dishes you'd see on fancy foodie blogs.

*[**food·ie** / ˈfo͞odē/ **noun**/ A person with a particular interest in gourmet food or more commonly in the social media era, the average person with access to a camera phone, a decent restaurant, and the food network.]*

The host led us through the kitchen into an outdoor oasis. Filled with lush landscaping and controlled open fire. We were seated at a fire pit and given the option of cannabis-infused or virgin cocktails. It was a no brainer. Once we finished our drinks, they seated us at a grand wooden chef's table. The head chef came out to let us know what we'd gotten ourselves into.

"Honored you guys could join us. What the team and I have prepared for you is a fifteen-course cannabis-infused meal with infused drink pairings. You can decide how many milligrams of THC you'd like depending on your tolerance level. We offer anywhere from ten to fifty milligrams. We have partnered with select top-shelf brands to gift you flower between courses. This is our way of protesting. The emergency shutdown has affected us all. Especially the people I consider my family in the hospitality industry. We coined cannabis hospitality as a term to introduce a more conscious culinary experience while de-stigmatizing plant medicine through food. We are excited to serve you. Thanks for coming, enjoy." And we did after selecting the highest possible THC dosage on the menu. You know the drill. No brainer.

  Each course was plated like a work of art, served to us like we were royalty, and tasted like it was cooked by God herself. Plates of smoked tuna on a radish tart and perfectly prepared Confit short rib served on a grapevine branch with Russian Kale, and Shallot Miso Ginger Bearnaise came one right after the other. Paired with incredible infused cocktails created to evolve as the meal goes on. Concoctions of St. George Gin, Maraschino Liqueur, blue pea flower, and juniper berries changed color with each new ingredient. Like a mood ring. The whole night was flawless. We laughed and carried on. I smoke courses off in-between. Fine dining in a cannabis-friendly community. This was my twisted version of heaven.

  The last three courses were dessert courses. Surprisingly, I wasn't full until the very last bite of the fifteenth course. Like the team studied the circumference of stomachs or something. Going into it, I wasn't sure how I would handle fifteen courses. I had difficulty getting through one course, but portions were small, and leaving a drop of sauce or grain of food on the plate seemed like a crime.

  We left in somewhat of a hurry. I was high, satisfied, and didn't want to do anything to fuck up a flawlessly executed night. The next day was a little foggy. Well worth it, but foggy. I was in disbelief that something so cool was right in my own backyard behind my back. That's the thing about L.A. there's always more to explore, experience, and fall in love with, even when you least expect it. When I asked Morgan if he misses the good old days. When you could illegally party in peace untouched by commercialism he simply responded,

> "It was the best of times, it was the worst of times."

America's Next Top Shooting

"In life, more than in anything else, it isn't easy to end up alive." -- Roman Payne

In a normal person's life, top models and drive-by shootings would never find their way into the same sentence. In my life, they went hand in hand. Sit tight; I can explain. After my short-lived year of lesbianism, our group of friends stood divided. Certain people fell out for individual reasons. One girl stopped paying the rent, so the other unfriended her. I chronically cheated on Kiely, so she unfriended me. She and her group members were now suing each other, so that friendship was overruled. I say all this to point out that all that, friends till the end, we knew each other since kindergarten crap is a bunch of bullshit. In real life, you lose just as many friends as you keep over the years, if not more. Friends shapeshift and change direction just as much as you do, and that's okay. Sisterhood of the traveling whatever, and every other young adult show and movie has tricked society into thinking that if you don't have four concrete girlfriends from the beginning of your life to the end of your life, you're doing friendship wrong. Nothing could be further from the truth. As obnoxious as it sounds, I've always had more friends than I can keep up with. I haven't felt like I fit in with all of them, but they were there.

One of my last friends standing is Sal. I got her in my hypothetical divorce from Kiely. She was technically Shawna's best friend, but since Shawna took it upon herself to inform Kiely of my infidelities, I suddenly had an opening for a best friend. Timing did its thing because Sal and Shawna wanted as little to do with each other as Kiely and I. Sal was sweet as fuck. Not a bad bone in her body. Physically she was about as close to biological perfection as one could get. Tall, slender, and stunning. She's Black and Spanish and most likely to be cast as the hot girl next door. Not the blonde playboy chicks that we'll get into later. The stereotypical girl next door. The natural beauty with a contagious smile and a cute little laugh. The kind of girl who makes a sports bra and yoga shorts look like an intentional ensemble.

Sal and I reconnected after years when we ran into each other in Vegas. It was All-Star weekend. Asia and I were both on the rebound. She was my play sister. For lack of a better word. I still can't remember which one of us convinced the other that Vegas was a good idea. Granted, everything in me hates everything about Las Vegas. I detest the loud carpeting in every hotel. I hate the girls wearing dresses that look like they're made out of Christmas tree tinsel. The recirculated air, the baseball cards with pictures of slutty escorts on them, the shitty music in clubs filled with people that could be extras on Jersey Shore, I can't stand any of it. What I could stand less was the thought of staying home to obsess over my ex-boyfriend and our decaying relationship. What's the worst that could happen? If something horrendous were to go down, no one would know anyway. Because of the whole, everything happening in Vegas staying in Vegas, law. It is a law, right?

Long story less long, Sal, Asia, and I all ended up at the same afterparty. Some mansion bash Lil Wayne was throwing after the game. Asia and I had been running from a group of swingers that were waiting on us hand and foot. At first, it was all good fun. We didn't realize that feeding us shots was just a step in their plan to seduce us. After eleven shots, we put two and two together. At around 2:00 am, we ran into Sal. We all screamed and hugged like we thought each other were dead until that exact moment.

We spent the following summer connected at the hip. Towards the end of the summer Sal called me in hysterics about having to go away. Not to boarding school or prison. She wasn't moving across the country or overseas. Sal auditioned and was selected to be on America's Next Top Model. She would spend the next few weeks in a "model house". Hence the dramatic rendition of I'm Leaving on a Jet Plane.

[mod·el house/ ˈmädl hous/ noun/ Sponsored housing where working models live in a group and vibrate at a more attractive frequency than the rest of us.]

The last few seasons of Top Model were filmed in faraway locations like Australia, so her concern wasn't fully unwarranted. She had no idea where they would be filming and enlisted me to go with her to say her goodbyes. We went on a Los Angeles County tour to see all her close friends and family. Her cousin, Quita, was my favorite and lived the furthest. There's no politically correct way to but this. Quita was hood as fuck. Rightfully so, you can't be posh with a name like Quita. There are basic elements of being hood that I always have and always will appreciate. Firstly, the jokes. The jokes are too good to ignore. The jokes are so good that they could carry my entire "why hood people are the best people" campaign. But I don't need it to—secondly, the brutal honesty. The truth has a habit of falling out of the hood's mouth. And I've always been a sucker for the truth.

I could go on forever, so let's end it with this. I love people from the hood. Quita is hood as fuck, and I love Quita. Basic math. She moved out to San Bernardino, which was nowhere close to the valley. A little over an hour away. Sal gave me fair warning that it would be a mission. We stopped at the gas station. Loaded up with snacks and hit the 210. Like clockwork, after an hour we were there. We weren't sure where exactly, but wherever it was, Quita was there.

Sal got out of the car,

"I think it's this one," she said, pointing to the house across the street.

"Just call her and see. It's cold." I was always cold.

Even in the summer. Something about low iron or anemia or something. Quita came running out of the house. Loud and hilarious.

"Biiiiiiiitch, I can't believe yall' valley asses came all the way up here." Quita convinced herself that we were snobbier than we actually were.

We followed her inside, and we weren't alone. I whispered,

"Quita, where are we?" as everyone watched us enter the house.

On a scale from not ghetto at all to pregnant bitches smoking weed, it was a ten out of ten. There were a couple of toddlers running through the smokey house. Quita pulled us into one of the bedrooms.

"Y'all know I'm in love, right? This Jason's house. He gon be here soon. My nigga is fine as fuck." Quita was giving us the Cliffs notes of what's been going on in her life.

"So, this is your boyfriend, Jason's house?" Sal inquired. She always sounded like an English teacher trying to make sense out of slang.

"Bitch yes, we gonna get married, we live together." There was no doubt in Quita's mind that she found the hood prince of her dreams. And they would soon move up to the eastside in a deluxe apartment in the sky.

"How many other people live here?" I asked.

"Nigga, I don't know. It just be me, Jason, his brother, Sharene, Mya, they kids, and his Momma, but she cool tho." Sal and I just listened and laughed at how animated she got while talking.

"My baby make money, and I'ma go-to cosmetology school..."

Quita couldn't get out the rest of her plans before Jason and his boys rushed into the house. Slamming the door behind them. They were all holding guns and talking a mile a minute. The energy shifted quickly. It was dark. Jason was tall. Ray Allen tall and looked like him a little bit too. He and his boys were all talking at the same time. "Nigga, I'll blow that niggas head off." "That's what they don't want." "I bust my whole shit fucking with those niggas." It was hard to make out who was saying what.

One of the aunties in the kitchen was making some of the best-fried chicken I ever had and shared in my frustration. "Jason, what the fuck is goin on? These sadity bitches don't need to be hearin' this shit" Apparently, that was Sal and me. We were the "sadity bitches." Jason explained that he and his boys were posted up when a group of niggas came and unloaded on them. Jason and his five boys were now loading guns in the living room.

"Wait, so you guys were just in a shootout, and you came straight here?" I asked.

"Yeah, but we gon see who bust last. I got somethin for them niggas." Jason's confidence is anything but comforting.

"We gotta go," I whispered to Sal. I liked Quita as much as the next chick, but these dudes practically handed everyone in that house over to their rivals on a silver platter. I've listened to way too much gangsta rap to get caught up like this. If I got killed in a shootout in San Bernadino, my parent's would fucking kill me.

"Y'all scary for real?" Quita played the guilt card. Why is it that everyone in the hood uses scary instead of scared? I've never been able to figure that mystery out.

"You should come with us." Quita looked at me like I had six heads and just asked her to join the church of Scientology.

Shots came flying into the house, and we all hit the floor like we'd done it before. I'm not sure if someone turned the lights off or they were shot out, but the house was not pitch black. Sal, Quita, and I army crawled to the bathroom. Several more shots flew in the windows of the house. At that moment, I mentally prepared myself to get shot. I started running through a list in my mind of people I knew that had been shot and survived. My ex, TK, was one of them. He'd been shot a lot, but he was a scrawny fucker. If he can take it, I can take it, I told myself. I had a dream I got shot in the hip a week before embarking on this San Bernardino excursion. When I woke up, I realized I just fell asleep on the remote. That's the closest I'd been to a bullet grazing my skin, and I was about to get a lot closer.

Quita started panicking. "Oh, my God. I don't wanna die. I don't wanna die. What do we do? What do we do?" Have you ever been scared for your life while simultaneously fighting the urge to repeatedly tell someone to shut the fuck up? Yeah, me too. Whispering shut the fuck up is no easy task. Especially when you can hear the footsteps of the guys that could end your life in seconds outside the bathroom window. I'm not sure if their guns had lights attached to them or if they had separate flashlights. But they were breaking windows and shining lights through them to see if there were any moving targets. Everyone was as still as a cemetery. I guess the shooters got impatient because they finally left.

We kept the lights off, and Jason explained that we couldn't leave yet. Due to the possibility of their opposition waiting outside to finish the job they started. We anxiously hung around for about an hour. Counting down the seconds until we could hit the 210 without looking back. The next day, Sal left to go compete and film America's Next Top Model. The model house was approximately 0.5 miles from her house. All that for nothing. The Long Kiss Goodnight scene just to come back and film in Studio

City. Just our luck. She ended up winning too. The Covergirl Contract, the prize money, the whole nine yards. She kept it a secret for months and didn't even tell me until the finale aired. Once she was crowned top model, our extracurricular activities changed from gunfire in the outskirts to sitting front row at Fashion Week. What a difference a day makes.

Billionaire Boys Club

"There are only two kinds of people in the world. The kind of people who think there's such a thing as enough money and the kind of people who have money." -- Fran Lebowitz

My ex and everyone else in our age group had suddenly developed a fascination for skate culture. And I developed a fascination for anything he developed a fascination with. This new cultural phenomenon didn't come out of the blue; it was ushered in by Pharrell Williams on a silver platter to mainstream hype-beasts for their viewing pleasure. I thought I'd gotten my affinity for skaters out of my system in middle school. Back when we would all wear DVS skate shoes just to watch the slackers grind rails between smoke sessions. But this was a more evolved version of the skater lifestyle we knew then. Apparently, with a lot more intensity because everyone was running around saying, "Skate or die, skate or die." They were still grinding rails and jumping stairs, but there was a new arrogant aesthetic involved this time around. There were grills and chains made up of VVS diamonds. Courtesy of Ben Baller and the fine folks at the Slauson Swap Meet. An Indoor shopping mall, smack in the middle of the hood for all your gaudy gold, fake jerseys, and sneakerhead needs.

Custom merch, VIP parties, and six-figure contest winnings were a given in the skate world now; X-games, street league, and world tours. Pharrell's super team of skaters was called

The Ice Cream Skate Team. Made up of five pro-skaters from all over the country. Sort of like the x-men but not.

There was whiteboy Jimmy, a goofy skater out of Philly with impressive taste in East Coast rap. Cato, Pharell's younger brother. He was around the least and the most difficult to get along with. Too smart for his own good with a permanent chip on his shoulder. Jacob was the youngest and arguably the best. He could land a switch inward heel tailslide on handrails before he was old enough to drive. K.B. was the cutest. From Carlsbad, California. The team captain brought him in—a street skater from the east side of Long Beach named Terry and called T.K. I'm not sure if it was his intention to garner the most attention, but it's hard to argue it wasn't. He played the token black skate rat "Compton Ass Terry" on Bam Margera and Rob Dyrdecks MTV series for however many seasons they ran. It never made much sense to me since he was from Long Beach and not Compton, but sometimes you have to tap dance for the check. That's just the way America works.

By the time I crossed paths with T, the Compton ass Terry dustiness had settled, and he was stepping into his own as Terry Kennedy. A semi-sophisticated version of the old him; If sophistication were ostentatious. Still a silly pro-skater, just one that dressed like a rapper that had signed their first deal. I met him at a club called Area. At least, it was called Area then. Before that, it was Night-N-Gale and before that Greystone. Now it's Greystone Nights at Night-N-Gale or something equally familiar and confusing. Every new club in L.A. is just an old club with a fresh coat of paint and a new name.

Terry's main focus then and now was everything pretentious. Image, money, clothes, cars, jewelry, women. Typical fast life at fuckboy high. The usual shit that men get strung out on. I'm not even sure he actually liked me. We said I love you after being together for so long; because it felt appropriate. It was more of an "I have love for you" thing. We just skipped a few words in the middle. To tell the truth, I could've been anyone that fit his sample size vision for the chick he came home to, and I knew it. A fuckin' cliche. Some pampered suburban priss, finally riding shotgun with a hood star smack dab in the middle of his fifteen seconds. Pathetic. Both drunk off the idea of fulfilling each other's fantasies and didn't even know it. We were too young to know better.

I was usually riding in his oversized, obnoxious car, or on his dick, which was the exact opposite. When he suggested a walk, it was out of the ordinary but sweet enough to consider. He turned to me in front of a fully bloomed rose bush and said he didn't believe that I would be with him if he didn't have money. I wanted to be insulted, but I felt bad for the guy. I felt bad that he was so used to that being the case that he suspected it was in all his relationships—even this one. I didn't have the heart to tell him that he didn't have as much money as he thought. He was able to get his grandma out of the hood and give his family a better environment, and I wanted him to continue to take pride in that. But he had no idea what real money was in this city. It isn't the guys that buy bottles at clubs, as he thought. Not the guys with the most chains and the sparkliest watch. Or the men that are overcompensating for their dick size with some flashy sports car. Real money in Los Angeles was a shit show of old money. And my middle-class ass had a front-row seat.

On Wednesdays and Sundays, Asia, Sal, and I were most likely to be found at The Staples Center. Wearing that horrendous yellow and gold combination and cheering on the home team. The owner's box wasn't half bad to a couple of twenty-somethings with time to kill: great drinks, great food, great seats. There wasn't much to complain about. Between quarters we'd go down to the shop and pick up a bunch of Lakers shit we didn't need because free something is better than nothing. I usually ended up sending it to out of town family that pedestal this place. When the game was over, we went to one of seven places. On Sundays, it was Dan Tanas. According to Jerry, it was a landmark Italian restaurant with some of the best steak on Santa Monica Blvd. He was a businessman and a poker enthusiast with a Ph.D. that happened to be the majority owner of a tiny sports organization called The Los Angeles Lakers. You may have heard of it. The last time I was at Dan Tanas, I saw Larry King walk in with a fucking smoke show. I'm talking drop dead gorgeous and all legs. Arm and arm with a Thumbelina of a man, he was this tiny little nerd that even I towered over. That's real money, I thought. Dan Tana's was one of the few places Jerry insisted on frequenting. It was an old Italian joint, but we went for their steak. For seventy-something, the guy sure could put a slab of beef away. I'm sure by now you're sinister mind has jumped to the conclusion that I was one of the youthful melanated girls that Jerry was fucking. Plot twist with a shocking turn of events, but I decided not to chuck my morals out the window for the sake of a good story. Not that time, anyway. My dad's worst nightmare would be to have some billionaire white guy, old enough to be HIS dad fucking HIS daughter.

I'd never been around anything like that before—elderly men with more money than God and a harem of twenty-somethings to choose from. You see shit like that a lot in L.A., Greying grandpas with pretty young things. But I'd never seen it up close and personal. All the girls knew about each other and accepted their place in the rotation. I couldn't believe it. It was like the daddy issues edition of musical chairs. There was Cortlin, the poster child for Orange County spray tans. Blonde from a bottle with dreams of being a Laker girl, Cortlin was nice enough to be a regular in the rotation. However, she wasn't high on the totem pole. Then there was Diana, an exotic knock-out from Vegas. I personally think she was Jerry's favorite, but her Muslim obligations complicated her availability. Not a good look for a man that needs his girls to be ready to pick up and go. Delia was my favorite. She didn't come around often, but when she did, she sure the fuck made sure you knew. Loud, brash, and unapologetic. The first time I met her, she was chasing Lil Jon around the player's lounge, pronouncing every missing letter of his name, and trying to convince him to talk to her brother on the phone,

"Little John, Little John, lemme take a picture dog. My brother loves you, fool," with a thick Spanish accent. Everyone else, for the most part, held their shit together no matter who stopped by.

Sometimes it was politicians, athletes, actors, etc. Delia didn't give a fuck about composure. It was thoroughly entertaining.

Another one of his regulars regularly brought her kid with her to the games. Rumor had it; her hyper-religious parents wouldn't allow her to have an abortion after being raped. I never fully put together whether or not she was one of Jerry's girls or if he was just dick deep in a superman complex. From what I could tell, the guy had a soft heart for a sad story. You'd have to be stone-cold for that tragic tale not to penetrate the surface. Lisa was the reigning champion of Jerry's attention. A Panamanian former Miss Tropic model who was the only one to finagle their relationship from romantic to platonic. If his personal life were a corporation. Lisa was the CEO. Everyone else was looking to move up in the company.

Jerry and his family were family-friends of Sal's, so she'd been used to the Anna Nicole antics. She'd been around it much longer, but it was all new to Asia and me. We'd have to excuse ourselves to the bathroom regularly to discuss the shit we couldn't believe our eyes were seeing. The open bar made witnessing the unbearable age gap more bearable. A round Mexican guy with a smile and a heavy hand named Carlos was the bartender. Most people had five or six cocktails throughout the night. We had an average of eleven. Still, not refined enough to have an impressive drink preference. Vodka, orange, and cran over ice got the job done.

It all became routine after a while. Wednesdays and Sundays were game days. Obligatory time to watch Kobe Bryant ball out while getting belligerent with my buds. Shit could be worse.

On Saturdays, Jerry would have the whole crew together for outings. The movies, brunches, USC games, dinners, clubbing. Eventually, you develop relationships. You can only be around the same group of people for so long without getting to know them. They weren't half bad. The girls were nicer to us than they were to each other. They knew that their positions weren't threatened, which automatically canceled us out of the competition ring. Jerry's son, Jesse, was around a lot with his boys, who were all our age. So it even began to feel like a normal group of friends. In L.A. terms.

On a normal night back in my normal life where women my age didn't date senior citizens, I was minding my own business, listening to The Black Album when I got a text. It was from Ed. Jerry's assistant. And read: Jerry would like to send a car for dinner. Ed didn't usually hit me up directly. Someone from their team would extend an invite to Sal, who would then extend an invite to me. I assumed that now that I'd become more of a familiar face, Jerry just wanted to make sure he knew who he had around.

The town car arrived a couple of minutes before 6:00 pm. Jerry was inside and alone, which I didn't expect. It was cool, though. I wasn't as uncomfortable around him now that I got to know him. We went to Flemmings in Marina Del Rey. He preferred to do most things in Marina Del Rey. The starting players in his harem all lived in condos in the same building in Marina Del Rey. He lived In Marina Del Rey, too, as did his star players.

Over dinner, we discussed all kinds of things—books, film, philosophy, sports, music. I tried to be on my best behavior, considering how hospitable he'd been without having any real idea of who I was or where I came from. After a few cocktails, I couldn't help it anymore.

"So what's up with all the dating way younger girls thing?" I blurted out. Jerry smiled and clapped his hands together like he was about to break it down. The complete opposite reaction of what I expected.

"Am I supposed to pretend that younger women aren't beautiful?"

he asked.

I hate when people answer a question with a question. He explained that he's seen it all and done it all. He continued on to say that he finds happiness in re-experiencing things with people who haven't experienced them yet. He also tap-danced around the generic excuse that all womanizers use.

"Women are the most beautiful creatures on earth," bla bla bla.

Do men actually think that we believe that load of crap? Yes, we know, women are fucking beautiful. I've fallen victim to it, myself. That does not, however, transform us into objects for men's amusement. I understand that it could be confusing. Most of the other shit men find beautiful are objects for their amusement. Cars, jewelry, clothes. Maybe it would help if men looked at women more in line with nature's beauty. The ocean, sunsets, mountainscapes. They're beautiful but not for you, just because. Appreciate it, don't abuse it. When you abuse true beauty, you automatically turn into an asshole. Without passing, go, to collect two hundred dollars. I mean, unless you're a part of the real billionaire boys club. I guess when you get enough money, ethics and morals are subjective.

The twisted part is, I didn't blame Jerry. He didn't have a malicious bone in his body. He said he knew these women were using him for money. He was also self-aware enough to cop to using them in return.

"As long as there are no secrets," he said.

Jerry went full throttle into a monologue about how women his age judge him for being himself, and younger women come with a freedom that he's accustomed to. He needs them to be able to pick up and go. We'd gone through two courses by this time, and the Crème brûlée just got to the table.

As I was dusting off the last of my brûlée in the tiny little ramekin it was served in, Jerry placed his hand on my leg. I tilted my head to the side and looked at him instead of saying

"of course," I said under my breath.

Which, of course, would have been my natural reaction.

I furrowed my brow, as to say,

"c'mon man, knock it off," except now I have a soft spot for the old man.

We had shit in common, and his perspective on things, albeit 50% bullshit, was interesting. Don't get me wrong; my soft spot had absolutely no effect on my common sense.

"C'mon Jerry; besides, I have a boyfriend," I said while wiping his hand off of my thigh. He rested this hand on his chin and looked up as if he were contemplating something.

"It's not something I would usually allow, but I might consider allowing that," he said. There was then a long pause. I was confused at his confusion. Typical male ego shit. The idea that I wasn't an option never crossed his mind. In his world, everything had a price. He'd never come across something he couldn't purchase in one way or another.

It made sense. A couple of weeks earlier, Jerry had Hugh Hefner by the box to watch the game. Naturally, he brought a flock of his blondies along with him. After a few drinks, finding out that they have a 9 pm curfew, are forbidden to have jobs, and only make $3000 a month, I started talking to them like they were underage strippers.

"You know you can make the same amount with a part-time job, right?"

I'd say to one.

"Why are you doing this?" I'd say to another.

"Don't you want to fuck someone your age at midnight because you can?"

I'd ask.

None of my advances penetrated the surface. These broads were playing the long game, and I guess I couldn't blame them. What the fuck else were they going to do?

The reality behind well off fossils chronically dating blossoming debutants is a lot less complicated than one might think. Most of these guys were too old to get it up, so dicking these young girls down was less on the agenda and more for the perception. But more than anything, this was about power. When it comes to wealthy men, it's always about power. They're all so drunk off money and power that they can hardly see straight. And the world marvels at their success, perpetuating their indecent behavior. The women have one thing on their side; time. They eventually live normal lives where they can shove their Anna Nicole aspirations deep down inside them. Never mentioning a word of it to their new husband. Happily ever after.

Summertime in the LBC

    "Fuck You for cheating on me. Fuck you for reducing it to the word cheating. As if this were a card game, and you sneaked a look at my hand. Who came up with the term cheating, anyway? A cheater, I imagine. Someone who thought liar was too harsh. Someone who thought devastator was too emotional. The same person who thought, oops, he'd gotten caught with his hand in the cookie jar. Fuck you. This isn't about slipping yourself an extra twenty dollars of Monopoly money. These are our lives. You went and broke our lives. You are so much worse than a cheater. You killed something. And you killed it when its back was turned."
    -- David Levithan

On a Summer night in Long Beach, anything is possible. On a Saturday night in 2005, my next ex learned that first hand. After attending a party on the east side, his party exit was interrupted with two shots. They both connected—one in the arm, one in the jaw. He was hit, and hard. Said he saw the bullets flying through the air in slow motion like the Matrix before they b-lined through his flesh. Said he got up and drove himself to St. Mary's Medical Center. Where he was hospitalized before making a full recovery, I wasn't there for any of this, of course. But niggas from the hood retell their dangerous triumphs about as often as white guys talk about their parents' divorce. Which is constantly.

    I can't prove that he was cheating on me our entire relationship, but if someone held a gun to my head, swearing they'd kill me if I guessed wrong, I'd have to say, probably. Dating a chronic cheater will turn you into a fucking psychopath. You're paranoid as all hell with trust issues like a back alley pit bull. One thing I think that most men have figured out is that all women in love have a tiny Russian hacker that lives inside of us. This doesn't mean that we rig elections or hoard Donald Trump's golden shower sex tapes. It simply means that since the beginning of the internet, and the dawn of social media, women will find out every microscopic detail about you. Who you are, who you want to be, who you're pretending to be. Your fetishes, your friends, your family, your fashion sense or lack thereof. Your grammar disabilities and toxic habits. Even if we can't find a likely answer, we'll just piece bullshit together until it resembles something believable. They call it women's intuition. Maybe it is. Maybe it's just being relentless as fuck about our nosey inhibitions.

  Surprisingly enough, my fuckboy and I were doing great, and I'd yet to dip into tricks of the trade. Primarily because he had just done thirty days in jail for brandishing a firearm. I guess gunplay hadn't put him through enough. Probation limited his ability to socialize. Subsequently, minimizing the opportunity to cheat on me. At least, that's the way my codependent and newly-blossomed-psychopathic-self saw it. We fell into our old routine. Spending every minute together when he wasn't working or skating.

  It would be months before I found out that to him, working and skating meant hanging out with a transplant socialite that doubles as a preacher's daughter behind my back. If you think that your boyfriend fucking someone else is an ego blow. Try finding out that your boyfriend is cheating on you and NOT fucking the girl. Does that even count as cheating? I know I sound naive, but "the other woman" was a bible banging virgin. She wasn't fucking anyone, let her tell it. And she did. Had this whole purity ring energy and wasn't quiet about it. I was getting dicked down on the regs by a dick that couldn't get hard if it were deep-fried, and he was secretly hanging from her tits like a newborn baby. I guess if it all happened today, you'd call it clout farming.

Her name was Angela, and as much as I wanted to hate her fuckin guts. She wasn't all that bad. Her dad was this iconic rapper turned reverend, and their whole family was subsequently quasi-known because of it. Real diary of a church girl shit. This was all public information. She and every other member of her immediate family had an MTV show that shoved their perfectly wholesome black excellence down everyone's throat. My mom didn't hate it, so I caught it in the wholesome crossfire when going from one room to another. Even when I didn't want to. Terry was on a couple of episodes and swore up and down they were "just friends" when I'd get the guts to question him about it. Not the most original excuse, but vague enough to get away with. His recent release allowed us a brand new start, a new start that distracted me from recognizing he was also getting a new start with her. Again.

I'd caught him fucking around before. We did the break-up to make-up dance so often it made me dizzy. I figured this time was different. He took me to his mom's grave and gave me some heartfelt speech that, in hindsight, was probably ripped off the screen of some sad hood movie. He came out of jail with muscles and a fresh appreciation for Christianity. Talking about how differently he sees life and how much he appreciated me. I figured it was well deserved. I had seen more than my share of mob movies while cultivating a shameless addiction to gangster rap since I was five, so playing the "down ass bitch" sort of came naturally. During his time, I'd drive down regularly to put money on his books, accept all the collect calls, talk to his team and lawyers to rally up for court dates like he was the center of the fucking universe. At the time, he was.

He found Jesus in there, like those that came before him as the good lord intended. He even slept with a Joel Osteen book next to the bed when he got out—pretending to read it before we'd fall asleep. This wasn't the womanizing fuckboy I cried over for thirty days. He'd grown in ways I never thought he could. This was a new and improved fuckboy. A fuckboy 2.0, if you will. One that I could love even more. With spiritual awareness, in the process of shattering his narcissistic tendencies. It was then that it hit me. An old dog can learn new tricks. I felt like the luckiest girl in the world. My man was free. He finally moved to the valley, about ten minutes away. Leaving all that street shit in the streets so that he could concentrate on skating, and me, of course. This man had come a long way from the pretentious prick that wouldn't take his sunglasses off at the dinner table.

Speaking of dinner tables, I was getting ready for a girl's dinner with my friend Ash. Technically, I got her in the Kiely break-up, like I did Sal. I guess I broke even in that situation. We both walked away with each other's friends and never looked back. Kiely and Ash were good friends until that friendship self-destructed. We reconnected because social media and life move on and bla bla bla. Ash lived in New York and was in town long enough for a quick catch up. Since the last time we saw each other physically, I was a pill-popping lesbian; there was much to catch her up on. We chose to meet at Robano's. A quaint pizza kitchen in Toluca Lake with a full bar and a dependable chef. Shawna had been working there, and it became sort of like our version of the Peach Pit. A retired mob boss named Ronnie ran the place. Nice man. Lived a long life. Ended up being taken out by that cunt, Cancer. I'm fairly certain it'll get us all.

I took the table near the garden plants and the rod iron fence and waited. Not the typical booth we claimed as our own, there weren't enough people for that this time. Just me and Ash trying to fit three years of life into two hours, a couple of cocktails, and a barbeque chicken pizza. She got straight to the point,

"Angela wants to hang, but I told her I was going to dinner with you, so..."

Did I mention that Ash is friends with the church girl socialite?

I never really knew the root of the friendship but assumed it was because they both did the reality TV thing in New York. The truth of the matter was that Angela and I didn't know each other from a can of paint. She didn't owe me shit. Granted, I'd been with the guy for the toxic part of two years, but we were perfect strangers until that night.

"Tell her to come," I said to Ash.

By the time Angela got there, I was half done with a medium pizza and two drinks past my limit. She skipped the small talk and an introduction, which I appreciated. I always have had a personal disdain for reciting meaningless truisms disguised as common courtesy. She walked in with Shawna, which should have been shocking but wasn't. Shawna was a regular on her spinoff show with Angela and her sister. So we were all there. Friends, enemies, frenemies; everyone was accounted for. She walked up to the table like Tiger Woods about to win the Masters.

"Did Terry tell you he was skating till nine tonight, too?" she blurted out before her ass hit the seat.

I didn't expect her to come in guns blazing. That's usually my approach. But I have to admit, I did respect it.

"Eight," I said, half in shock, half stupid. I'm not sure if she rehearsed this, but she had the next part down perfectly.

"Look, I don't want to go back and forth with the he-said, she-said, so do you just want to switch phones so we can figure out who's telling the truth?" she said, extending her arm across the table, handing me her unlocked phone. I wanted to say something condescending and bitchy. But couldn't. This was the best idea I'd heard in months.

I unlocked my phone and handed it over. We went straight to each other's text messages and let the Russian hacker within go crazy. After endless scrolling and comparing notes, we got down to the bottom of it. Fuckboy 2.0 had been texting us the same exact messages for the last two months. If he sent me a message saying,

"I love you, wifey, she means nothing to me" At 8:00 pm.

He would copy/paste it and send her the same text at 8:01 pm. This was the case for damn near every text he'd sent us. The only time he deferred from the strategy was when we asked him something so specific he had to address it individually. It was official. This was easily one of the top ten stupidest times of my life.

We tossed back some drinks and ordered some bruschetta to soak up the alcohol. The dinner went from a catch up with Ash. To a tell-all with Ang, and now a think tank with Ash, Shawna, and Angela on, how to handle this piece of shit. When I say handle, I don't mean handle handle. I said I've watched a lot of mob movies. I didn't say I'm delusional enough to live them out. We just had to figure out a way to embarrass him the way that he embarrassed us. We should've been heartbroken, looking to resolve the matter with grace and dignity. If it happened closer to today, we probably would've handled it that way. Then we were young, petty, and our pride hurt worse than our hearts.

The plan was to wait for him to call one of us. Then to reveal that we were together. I'd be lying if I said it wasn't a pissing contest to see who he'd call first. Part of me knew it would be her. At 8:07, my phone rang.

"Hey," I said like nothing was up.

"I'm on my way home; where you at?" Terry said like he would have any other day.

"Oh, I'm still at dinner," I responded.

"Who you with?" he asked. The conversation was going as it would if I weren't about to take the wind out of his metaphorical sails.

"Me, Ash, Shawna, Angela..." I waited for a response.

"Oh, nobody, I know? How long you gon be?" he asked.

"Yeah, you know Angela, I don't think you know the other two. I really can't call it," I said.

"Wait, Angela, who?" finally, a tone of worry, exactly what we were looking for.

"That's right, Terry, you're caught bitch!" Angela screamed into the speaker of the phone. Terry hung up immediately.

"Did he hang up?" she asked.

"Of course he did," Shawna said.

"What else was he gonna do?" A few minutes later, Angela's phone rang. We both took turns screaming disrespectful as soon as she picked up. Terry hung up again. Not before saying,

"fuck y'all." That's just the kind of guy he was. Possibly still is. I wouldn't know.

We spent the rest of our time at the Italian eatery assuring and reassuring each other that neither of us would take him back. Not under any circumstances. We pinky promised like children and drank to it like adults. Flipping off the camera while the girls snapped pics for us to plaster on our social accounts. If for nothing else, to rub salt in the wound. To be honest, I figured she'd crack. I thought she'd take him back, and the two of them would do the media darling thing all over again. I made peace with that possibility before I left that night. I knew my pride would stop me from ever speaking to him again. I also learned that most women don't operate that way. I didn't even plan on holding it against her. If she took him back, she probably deserved to be with a guy like that. In the same way, it would be what I deserve if I did.

Angela Simmons and Brenn Colleen go 'Two Can Play That Game' on Terry Kennedy. At Least that's what the headline on random trash websites and gossip bloggers said. I thought that getting the last laugh would soothe the humiliation. I was wrong. Ang and I went our separate ways. Both, holding up our end of the deal. We wound up at the same after-party a few times. On slow news days, those same bored bloggers ate that shit up. Spinning some story about how we were BFFs to get back at him. I guess that was when I learned how full of shit the media can be. We weren't even friends, let alone best anything.

I didn't speak to T.K. again after that. Until he showed up on my doorstep in Toluca Lake two years later. I wouldn't let him in the house, and spoke to him through the screen like a door to door salesman. He must've gotten the alert that all exes get when you move on. I lived there with my new man, and he was due home any minute. Terry fed me an ear full about how I was the one, and my current boyfriend was just with me because he was copying him. That he was a trendsetter, and he'd been through hell and back. It was the same song he'd been singing since I met him. All I could think was change the station, I hate this song. Mental illness sure can be a son of a bitch.

You Know You're a Native

> *"See, that's the thing about L.A.— When you've mastered the art of feeling lonely in a room full of people, that's when you know."* -- Kris Kidd

You know you're a native if you don't flinch when there's an earthquake under 4.0.

You know you're a native if you consider three days of juicing a solution to a summer of binge drinking and taco Tuesdays.

You know you're a native if you acknowledge the Oscars, the LA Marathon, or a Dodger game as equal forms of traffic terrorism.

You know you're a native if you consider gay pride a national holiday.

You know you're a native if you know how to pronounce Sepulveda, La Cienega, Doheny correctly.

You know you're a native if animal fries are one of your guilty pleasures.

You know you're a native if you would rather drink a glass of hot sand than be caught on the PCH during a holiday weekend.

You know you're a native if you say you're on your way before you've left your house.

You know you're a native if one of every three people you know is vegan or gluten-free.

You know you're a native if you consider a high speed chase an extreme sport.

You know you're a native if you live as if public transportation doesn't exist.

You know you're a native if you think, there better be an accident, when traffic slows down.

You know you're a native if "road trip" means you'll end up in Palm Springs, Joshua Tree, or Vegas.

You know you're a native if you call an Obama special a number nine with a waffle.

You know you're a native if you ever took a field trip to the La Brea Tar Pits.

You know you're a native if any temperature below Sixty-Five Degrees means you can pull out your winter wardrobe.

You know you're a native if you have a growing collection of crystals.

You know you're a native if you bring mace on night walks.

You know you're a native if you've used someone else's Westside Rental account.

You know you're a native when orders off secret menus become routine.

You know you're a native if you say you're on your way before you've left your house.

You know you're a native if you can get to LAX without the 405.

You know you're a native if a stranger has approached you just to tell you they love your energy.

        You know you're a native if 'unfuckably nice' is a valid reason not to date someone.

You know you're a native when you consider laying out a full day's work.

You know you're a native if brunch is your most practiced sport.

You know you're a native if you speak just enough Spanish to bargain park.

You know you're a native if you spend more time in your car than anywhere else.

        You know you're a native if you avoid Hollywood and Highland like the plague.

You know you're a native if you consider Earthquake, Santa Ana Wind, Fire, and Mudslide the four seasons.

You know you're a native if you've driven an hour to have a legal bonfire on the beach.

You know you're a native if you don't have to use Waze to take alternative routes when traffic comes to a halt.

You know you're a native when animal style is a part of your In-N-Out order.

Road Rage

"I drive kinda recklessly, I take a lot of chances, I never repair my vehicles, and I don't believe in traffic laws. So I tend to have quite a high number of traffic accidents. And last week I either ran over a sheep, or I ran over a small man wearing a sheepskin coat." -- George Carlin

Have you ever met somebody so bad at driving that they set women back? It's me; I'm that somebody. I once read a quote saying there are essentially three types of drivers in Los Angeles: competent, overcautious, and reckless. Beneath all the road rage, I'd say I teeter between competent and reckless, depending on what time of the day you ask. My issue is that I never give myself enough time to get where I'm going, and if I do, the music I'm listening to is so good it's distracting.

There's a special place in hell for overly cautious drivers. Somewhere a fairy loses its wings every time they buckle up. Those are the people who drive half the speed limit at all times and take fucking forever to make a left-hand turn. When passing a cautious driver, after they've tested my patience for a few blocks, I make a point to look them directly in the eye—scowling my face off hard as hell. If they aren't visibly over the age of 70, it infuriates me even more than their sluggish driving. If they return the same energy, I begin to mouth "We can get out" as if they're professional lip readers. The rage takes over logic, and I temporarily forget how stupid angry people look in traffic.

Reckless drivers are usually young, old, drunk, intoxicated, and sometimes three out of the four. The only reckless drivers who are none of the above are only ever one thing. Eternally late. Driving in a rush to make up for the time we never had. Maybe we had it, but we fucked up our eyeliner one too many times, and the extra time we did have disintegrated with every wipe of a q-tip and liquid stroke. It's a classic recipe for disaster. One that women know well. One that I know better than most.

It's said that if you can drive in Los Angeles, you can drive anywhere. One thing unaccounted for is that no one in L.A. can actually drive. The worst drivers out there are hands down, tour bus drivers. These Topless vans are owned and operated by Inadequate shitty drivers that give tourists a glance at celebrity homes. I'd rather drink my own piss than be stuck behind one of those in one of the canyons. It's pure torture and happens more often than one would think.

I was taken hostage behind one in Outpost Canyon a couple of weeks ago. I contemplated homicide a total of four times before I got to Franklin Ave. The bus didn't have not one passenger and insisted on driving slower than the hiking pedestrians. I slammed my hand on the horn and kept it there the entire time. An ongoing, obnoxiously loud "HOOOOOOOOONK!" scored every twist and turn of the canyon. No one likes the person that lays on their horn. I can't even stand that person. But that's what L.A. traffic does to you. It turns you into the people you hate.

I headed west on Franklin towards La Brea. The bus was now on the left-hand side of me. I glance over at the driver. Fully prepared to burn a hole in his soul with my eyes. My music was on max, and the windows were rolled up, so I couldn't hear him, but he was going to town. Screaming obscenities, flipping me off. He looked like a flamboyant meth-addicted version of one of those Sons of Anarchy guys. Long hair, gross teeth, and a beard that you could light a match on. The traffic light at La Brea and Franklin went from yellow to red at the most inopportune time. Sons of Anarchy was right next to me at the light. I hated for him to think thatI gave a fuck about his driver seat theatrics, so I rolled down my window and mouthed,

"I can't hear you". Which was a blatant lie;

I could make out perfectly what he was saying, and I was fully committed to the dumb bimbo act I was putting on. I learned in traffic that when you act too stupid to insult, it pisses people off even more. And if you never got the rules to the road rage game, let me help. Whoever drives off least angry wins.

Match beard had now been yelling about how much of a bitch I am for two and a half city blocks. I turned my music down.

"I can smell your cunt from here, you stupid bitch" he screamed before burning rubber as he peeled off.

I couldn't help but laugh for a few reasons. I didn't catch it at first. But my gaydar has never misled me. This dip shit may look like a Harley Davidson reject, but inside there was a RuPaul's Drag Race binge-watching power bottom dying to get out. It isn't every day you hear a straight guy slang the word cunt around so casually. I've always been a fan of the slur, but American's usually thought of it as going too far when you'd toss it in your everyday vernacular. I respected it. As offensive as the flamboyant Viking intended on being, he was fuckin hilarious. Only in L.A., I thought.

Not all road rage encounters leave you with a smile. Although, if you go into them smiling, it's hard not to keep it up.

About a week prior, I pulled into a parking lot for a routine caffeine fix. Nowhere special, just 7/11 per usual. After catching up with Rohit, the cashier, on how much he missed his wife in Sri Lanka, I dipped out of the convenience store caffeine in hand. Between me and my car was an old lady, not grandma old, but somewhere between your mom and grandma. She looked a bit like an anorexic Kathy Bates without the talent and was screaming racist shit that sounded like she meant to say it under her breath.

"I can't stand it. These niggers are everywhere," she repeated.

Then walked directly up to me and said,

"Do you see them? They're everywhere. These niggers are everywhere."

Now, in her defense, the parking lot was randomly poppin'. I'd say a parking lot that the store staff and I are typically the only people of color in, that day had maybe four cars with black drivers or passengers. That was four too many for racist Kathy. The fact that she came up to me and looked me right in my face before asking me if I was aware the parking lot was overflowing with niggers, is what confused me most.

"You do realize I'm black, right?" I said in a dry tone of voice.

"Listen, honey, you and all your friends need to get out. Why don't you just go back to Africa?" she said. I looked around to see if I was being punked. No hidden camera crews came out—no Ashton Kutcher or Chance the Rapper insight.

"Are you paying? I've been dying to go to Africa." I responded. It was clear that this woman didn't have two nickels to rub together. Something I'm usually sensitive to, but her racist fuckery canceled out my sensitivity, and rightfully so.

"I've made more money than you'll ever see in your nigger life," she said, barefooted on the concrete.

"Yeah, I can tell," I responded.

At this point, I knew I should walk away. This broad had a screw loose, and I knew that arguing with fools is a fool's game. I proceeded to open the door of my car. What was there left to say?

"My sons are more successful than your whole family. We can buy a ticket for every nigger you know to take your black asses back to Africa," her facial expression showed that she was pretty damn proud of that last line.

She squinted her eyes to really drill in that she was dead serious. I almost wanted to let the broke bitch have it. To let her take the win. She looked like she could use a win. Then the petty bitch that lives inside of me tied up all my common sense and did her thing. Besides, where do these nut jobs get off? I'll be honest, I'm not the sanest person I've ever met, and mental health is a serious issue, but are the racist overtones a necessary additive to this bitches preferred brand of crazy?

"Cool, can you make sure to book my ticket a couple weeks out? I want to find your sons first so I can fuck them and turn your whole family black." I said before smiling and closing my car door behind me.

Racist Kathy Bates looked at me like she couldn't believe I could say something so evil. I knew I shouldn't have carried on with her. I shouldn't have dignified any of the baseless bullshit she was spewing with a response. I should've channeled my inner Michelle Obama. When she went low, I could've gone high. It's just not who I am. I'm more of an if you go low, I'll meet you there type of girl. There's plenty of things I'm willing to disagree with people about. Racism doesn't happen to be one of them. If there's a problem with that, feel free to find me in traffic.

A more recent run-in with road age was earlier this year. I'd left my office early, and was on my way home to grab an overnight bag before heading to my boyfriend's place. Like every warm-blooded girlfriend that gets off work early. I had my phone on my lap mid facetime with Ash. We were discussing a docu-series we've been developing for the past two years when I noticed a cop in my rear-view mirror. I immediately slowed down—rookie mistake. O waited for the lane to break and exited the freeway immediately. Some cops would call this suspicious activity. I'll level with you; I was scared out of my fucking mind. I've always had anxiety when it came to dealing with the police. I once had an NYPD cop try to finger me when he was "checking for sharp objects," so forgive me if I lack a little composure when they're in close proximity.

My freeway exit was erratic. So when the siren rang and the lights flickered, I wasn't surprised. I was already shaking. Pulling over felt like it would be in everyone's best interest. I pulled into the nearest driveway, turned the engine off, and waited. The whole time, hysterically narrating what was going on to Ash while begging her to stay on the phone. She did.

I was waiting for the officer to approach my window. To hit me with their smash hit, "license and registration." But there was nothing.

No double knock on my window. No unnecessary flashlight shining in my eyes. I glanced in my side-view mirror to see the officer standing behind his wide-open car door for cover while pointing a gun the size of my arm directly at my car.

"Everybody out of the car!"

"Everybody out of the car!" he repeatedly yelled.

Unsure about what could have triggered him to respond so aggressively, I had no choice but to resort to my "worst-case scenario plan."

[Worst Case Scenario Plan - For Emergencies Only]

Step 1: Retrieve cherry Nyquil from the center consult.

Step 2: Open the bottle and dip two of your fingers directly into the Nighttime Relief medicine.

Step 3: With the same hand, unbutton and unzip your pants. Leaving residue from the cough suppressant syrup.

Step 4: Dip a napkin or Kleenex in the syrup as well before opening your car door to exit, act embarrassed and leave the rest to God.

By the time I finished all four steps, and trust me, I did them as quickly, and with as little movement as possible, the cop was not approaching my car. With one eye closed for better aim, he was now standing outside of my window with his gun cocked.

"Everybody out, and on the ground!" He yelled while pointing his gun at the driver's side window. I opened the door.

"On the ground, everybody on the ground," he continued to scream. I wasn't sure who everybody was.

"On the ground now. Everybody out!" he continued to repeat.

I got out and on the ground, with my all Nyquil everything drip aesthetic. The officer went around opening all four doors to make sure no one else was in the car. I continued to lay on the ground. I could hear his steps getting closer.

"Hands behind your back!" he screamed with his gun pointed at my back.

I removed my hands, placing them behind me with the bloody Nyquil napkin.

"I'm sorry, I just started my period; I just need to find a bathroom," I said. The cop immediately got uncomfortable and began to stutter once he looked down and saw the blood on my hands and pants.

"Okay, um, clean, clean, just, clean up, and I'll turn away," he said.

It was obvious that he was ready to wrap up the interaction after menstruation entered the equation. Nothing makes a man uncomfortable, like a bloody pussy. He gave me a ticket for a California stop at the exit before telling me that he thought I was in a stolen vehicle and on my way to a police chase.

Less than three months later, The Black Lives Matter Uprising would get a resurgence due to the alarming rate of footage circulating of the unjust murders. Every time a female victim's picture made the press, I'd sit up that night wondering why I didn't die that day, on that ground, by that cop. I fit the mold. Black at all is black enough. I wonder if it was because I was clever with a plan B or well-spoken when questioned. Maybe because that unnecessarily aggressive officer hated menstruation more than he hated a minority driving a nice car. Whatever the answer, at least I'm here to wonder about it. A lot of people that look like me weren't granted that privilege. Hello white America, assassinate my character.

The Crazies

"There are bad people in the world: Murderers and psychopaths and telemarketers who won't take no for an answer." -- Jennifer Lynn Barnes

All my life, I've been called crazy. So much so that I halfway started to believe it. "You're so crazy." The standard response from the majority of my friends when I say something that they wouldn't. The other day I did a podcast where the hosts asked me the craziest thing I'd ever done. I never know what to say when someone asks me that. Guys always ask on first dates, and I typically say. "A lot," which is my lazy way of answering honestly while keeping it simple. You'd think that flipping off the 405 freeway, sneaking to a dessert party when I was thirteen, hitchhiking to get my tongue pierced, or surviving the Northridge earthquake would come to mind, but it never does.

"Um, does skydiving count?" I asked.

"Hell yeah, it counts," host #1 responded.

They are both named Ashley because they were born in the '80s, and it's easier to refer to them as host 1 and 2.

"You've done that?" Host 2 asked?

"Yeah, you haven't?" I asked.

"Get the fuck out of here; I'm black for real," host 1 said.

"I guess I'm not," I said sarcastically.

"No, you are, but you know you're crazy," she said.

The one thing that both hosts and I could all agree on is that I was a little crazy.

"But not crazy-crazy, cute-crazy, right?" I asked.

*[**Cute-crazy/ kyo͞ot/ ˈkrāzē/ adjective/** Someone who is triggered emotionally, and responds in toxic and irrational ways, while being cute enough to get away with it.]*

*[**Crazy-crazy / ˈkrāzē/ ˈkrāzē/ adjective/** Mentally deranged, especially as manifested in a wild, aggressive or sinister nature.]*

Someone who is crazy-crazy will kill your whole family and eat pancakes afterward as nothing happened. Someone who is cute-crazy will pour red Gatorade all over your shoe collection or hack your social media account because you hurt their feelings. There's a distinct difference.

I like to think that I grew out of that crazy-shit, but I guess you'll have to ask my man. The point is, there's a lot of breeds of crazy out there.

You never realize how someone else's preferred brand of crazy can affect your life until it does. It interrupts the middle of your workday with no regard, like a natural disaster.

I ran out of a meeting like a worried mother when I got the call that Joey was stabbed and in critical condition at Cedars Sinai Medical Center. The same hospital my brother was born at. My mom used to make a joke that it was the reason he likes Jewish women. But that was when you could say shit like that. Things weren't funny anymore. The guy I could always count on to make me laugh was in pain, and I couldn't do a damn thing about it. I made up some bullshit lie about how my brother was in an accident. I guess it could be true if you look at it in one of those, we're all God's children, kind of ways.

I rushed through the emergency doors as if my daughter had just been raped. Worry all over my face and a lump of urgency in my throat "I'm looking for Joseph Ryan La Cour; he's my twin brother." Another lie, but this was no time to toy with technicalities. Emergency informed me that Joey was no longer in there and was now recuperating in the Intensive Care Unit. The doctors in the ICU explained that his liver was punctured when he was stabbed. Did I mention he was stabbed?

The night before, Joey, Julien, Karrueche, and a flock of our friends took to the night. After the party was the after-party, landing them at some hilltop mansion where The Weeknd was celebrating the collection of trophies he racked up at the award show earlier in the evening. Everything was going as it should. R&B thugs and their teenage mutant model girlfriends, Soundcloud rappers with that vacant look in their eye that says Will Work for Percocets, Youtube douches, and internet gamers that make more money than all of the above combined. Last and least, an L.A. party wouldn't be a party if there weren't a healthy helping of chicks that get wet at the thought of being around celebrities and dudes that get hard for the same reason. They were all accounted for.

Joey and the gang grew bored of the celebration and decided it was time to head out. Walking towards the door, they had no idea what they were walking out of or into. On the other side of that door stood a crowd bitter with the fear of missing out. Sounds stupid, but not getting into a party after getting all dressed up does something to people like you wouldn't believe. A guy with a short man's complex named Will let his party blue balls get the best of him. Deciding to test his luck with security. Resulting in getting cracked over the head with a bottle. Just a casualty of after-party war. Somewhere between getting a champagne bottle smashed on his skull and Joey and company making their exit, paths crossed at the wrong time. Will was on the loose with a knife in hand and retaliation on his mind. On the hunt for the security guard that humiliated him in front of the party.

The door finally swung open, and Will thought he had the gigantic enforcer where he wanted him. He plunged forward, jamming his blade right into his chest before running off. Except it wasn't the security guard. It was Joey. Who didn't understand what the fuck just happened? He took a step back, and his knees gave out a little. Julien reinforced him.

"Are you good?" Karrueche asked.

"Yeah, that kid just punched me," Joey said while putting his hand over his chest.

Realizing there was a hole and his hand was covered in blood. Will, The psychotic fuck, let his party blue balls take him to a place so dark that he was willing to take the life of someone he didn't even know. Now here I am in the hospital conversing with medical staff about whether or not my best friend's liver is going to be able to heal itself or whether he'll require surgery. For a night out. For a fucking night out.

Joey said later that he'd seen that guy Will around before. He said that he seemed like a quiet dude. I guess you never know who the real crazies are in this town. They blend right in with the rest of us. That wasn't the first time Joey unintentionally let the crazies get too close for comfort.

    Hagen was a Kentucky boy that Joey started bringing around a few summers ago. He spoke with a southern twang and was always hospitable and charming. I never really knew what Hagen did. Just another nice guy whose sexuality we all ignorantly questioned because of his recent bromance with Joey. Hagen was handsome and as straight as an arrow. Our interactions were few, far between, and usually unintentional. He moved away after trying his hand in L.A and that was that I never really gave it a second thought. This place and the industries that live in it are a revolving door. People come in. People go out. It's more surprising when people stay than when people go back home.

    Whenever Joey would bring Hagen up in casual conversation, I'd tell him that he's forever burned in my memory as the kid who got me for my pipe. Hagen smoked weed, which always went over well whenever I'm personally evaluating someone. It also came in handy, considering I was in the middle of a high alert emergency. That's code for; I ran out of weed. Hagen barely had any, but barely was more than I had. Negotiations were now in order. I presented my offer. Told him that he could keep my pipe if, in return, he gave me some weed. It seemed like a no-brainer at the time. I was a blunt smoker, anyway. The pipe was purely for break the glass emergencies. Hagen kindly accepted the terms of my generous offer, and we traded. My indica withdrawals were put to ease by the sweet inhaling of some good old fashion O.G. Kush. Hagen had a new pipe that had only been used twice, and everyone was happy. I didn't see him much after that.

Last I heard, he moved home, met some chick, and had a baby. Of course, that information came by word of mouth from Joey. I imagined him to be one of those southern charm dads. One that wears a cowboy hat like Ryan Gosling in Nothing Too Good for a Cowboy. Surrounded by haystacks, somewhere back in Kentucky. Living the white picket fence life.

When the CNN headline made its way to the top of my algorithm, you can imagine my surprise. Hagen Mills, 'Baskets' actor, dead at 29, it read. My first thought was... wait, Hagen was an actor? My second was that it had to be a tragic freak accident. Maybe a drunk driver hit him, or he tried to drive after one too many. Possibly a plane crash, unintentional overdose, or undiagnosed cancer. Any of these would have been more believable than the truth. I stopped spitballing about what it could be and bit the clickbait.

Hagen Mills, an actor who appeared in the television series, *Baskets died Tuesday after allegedly shooting the mother of his young daughter, according to police in Mayfield, Kentucky. Mills was 29,* the headline, and subtext read.

Straight to the point and unfuckingbelievable. The piece continued on to discuss, in detail, how Hagen attempted to shoot his baby's mom dead before blowing a few holes in himself. Unexpectedly, the woman survived, with a shot to her arm and through her chest. The silver lining to the story was that the daughter got out unscathed. That is unless you count the endless years of therapy, abandonment issues, and traumatic PTSD. The story was all over the news. I guess Hagen was known for more than finessing handblown glass pipes from unsuspecting friends. Who knew?

It just goes to show you. You never know somebody until you know somebody. When I take a step back and look at life, trying to pick out all the psychopaths that crossed my path in this place; It still gives me chills. I wish I could say I never knew anyone that could do something so evil, but that would be absolute bullshit.

In high school, there was this guy named Charles that used to pal around with a few of my dude friends. He was kind of a lackey for lack of better words—quiet, demure, dying to fit in. I lost touch, and it was hard to keep tabs on most of them when real life set in. But not Charles, I would have had to be immune to headline news for that. Local newscasters informed me and the rest of their viewership that Charles was now an accessory to group murder. Long story short, he's said to have helped his friend kill his girlfriend's family. Rumors swirled that it was because the girlfriend was Muslim and her family didn't want her dating a kafir. Which is basically Arabic for not Muslim. I'm not sure where, when, or how Charles and his boy decided that a plausible solution to the problem was to kill all involved, but allegedly they did.

IT ONLY SEEMS RANDOM

It's hard to imagine an unsure kid committing a homicide. This is the same guy that got his jaw broke and wired shut for the entirety of the sophomore year. How do you decipher who has that missing chip in their conscience? Or differentiate who's capable of committing one of the only universal sins we can all agree upon. I rack my brain trying to figure out how many blunts, or car rides, I've shared with psychopathic murderers in my life. How many times I've hugged one without knowing that their future was bloody and soulless. Or maybe even gave one a tongue lashing on a bitchy day without realizing they were sparing me from total slaughter.

It isn't just people in passing or outcasts that do these things. Not in Los Angeles. Here, you can be anyone, and that makes the perfect canvas for the crazies. For some, it's beautiful and picturesque for the beautiful and picturesque. For others, it's a facade. On the flip-side of a sunny day, it's dark as midnight and dangerous as fuck.

Kevin was the big man on campus. Brilliant at football. Better at girls, with a smile that could kill. And it did. He did what Hagen did about six months before he did it. The only difference is, when it was all said and done, Hagen was too dead to give a damn that his girl survived. Kevin didn't get so lucky. His shots did what they were meant to do. Ripping through the flesh of his lover and taking her life. He didn't have the same precision when he turned the barrel of the gun on himself. Today he's holed up somewhere with brain-damage. He's likely being fed and bathed, and reliving the day he took the life of the woman he loved. I gues psychopath.

Part Three - The Coast

Don't Panic, It's Organic

"Prison is for rapists, thieves, and murderers. If you lock someone up for smoking a plant that makes them happy, then you're the fucking criminal." -- Joe Rogan

If I had a dollar for every weed guy that's come in and out of my life, I'd never need to work again. Let's see; there was Mumbles from Pasadena, Pimp Player from Calabasas, Ethan and Matt in Chatsworth, Brandon and Aaron in the same place. The two Chris' in Long Beach, Shaggy, and Bently in Hollywood. Ed in the hills. Two blunt Antoine could meet you anywhere but was usually downtown. The best weed guys are always new weed guys. When they've met you and still have no idea that you'll never fuck them, that's when they're on their best behavior. They'll charge you next to nothing and throw in all kinds of extra shit. It's a win-win. An extra eighth here and some edible gummy bears there. They'd even bring the weed to your front door like pot valet before delivery dispensaries existed.

The sad reality is that the ancient art of slanging weed is a dead art form. It was fun while it lasted, but it's 2021, and convenience and tech are giving the lazy world what it deserves. We can get our herbal refreshments in-store, from apps, in swag bags at parties, by clicking our heels together three times and saying, Mary Jane. In Los Angeles, it's harder not to get weed than it is to get it. My affinity for that skunky flower started young. Too young to inhale appropriately. I remember laughing a lot and coughing more. I tried to roll and smoke countless joints throughout my early teenage years but failed miserably. There really is a science to it.

It wouldn't be until I was out of high school that I'd smoke my first blunt. It was something like a right of passage when I was hanging out with my dude friends, Katrell, Aaron, and Brandon. We'd smoke the day away and laugh our asses off while watching The Chappelle Show over and over. If we weren't doing that, we were hotboxing Aaron's Nissan Altima and religiously listening to Jay-Z. All in a day's work. I hate to say that went on for years, but that went on for years. Cementing my undying appreciation for three things: Everything Dave Chapelle, Jay-Z, and an unconditional love for Marijuana. Specifically Indica. Preferably, O.G.

I nursed an on-again-off-again relationship with weed right into adulthood. I'd smoke more mid wrapped up in a peach Optimo than I should have. In my defense, I was too young and too broke to know better.

*[**MID / mid/ adjective/** Short for mid-grade weed. It's not the best weed and not the worst, but just kind of in the middle.]*

My twenty's brought me two things; A lot of bullshit and top-shelf weed to smoke off the bullshit. The gross part is, I was smoking commercial blunts. They're basically the chicken McNuggets of weed-smoking vehicles. No one really knows what's in them; we just take them to the face—knowing only that they're blended up real well somewhere in some factory and smoothed out entirely until the ingredients are undetectable like a chicken McNugget, or a hot dog, or something.

Between the mid-shelf tree and the blunt wraps, I was doing my pot fetish a real disservice. I added fuel to the fire by developing a pretty intense addiction to backwoods in the years to follow. By the time my friend Somerset asked me to come up north and visit her in the grow she'd been working in, it seemed like a tempting idea to toss around. Unbeknownst to her, I was in the beginning stages of writing a satire about women in cannabis called "You Grow Girl." The offer came at the perfect time. What's better than a little hands-on experience? The truth is, I could use the extra cash. My last staff writing gig fell through months ago, and my savings account was losing too much weight. Somerset was one of those students of the universe types. She reads tarot cards, makes organic lotions, and knows all that extra shit about astrology; when what moon aligns with what planet, and what it means. Running a grow was right on-brand for her granola ass.

She said she'd been making a ton of money and had more weed than she could physically consume. Okay fuck it, we talked me into it. Working in a grow means early mornings, and I don't just mean 8 am school days or 9 am staff meetings. I'm talking, up before the sun is, every fucking day. Up and out while it's still dark, cold, and wet from the night before. Not my idea of a good time. If it were up to me, I'd sleep all day and write all night. I knew I signed up for something I might not be equipped to handle. The abandoned warehouse was in the Acorn projects in Oakland and used to be a bank or some financial institution with multiple bank vaults. They would lock us in that bitch until sundown like solitary. Do you know how much weed you can trim in a twelve-hour day? Approximately two pounds. Three if you have a reliable Adderall supply. Which I didn't, until my second day. Five if you slept there. At $150 a pound, it seemed worth it, but Somer was a different kind of animal.

  The security system was the only impressive thing about that place. It was run by this frail chick that looked like she could've been an early cast member on Teen Mom, named Christina and her idiot brother, Tim. Heroin and Mountain Dew had to have been their babysitter cause it showed. It's easy to grow shitty weed, and they did it with pride. I wasn't like Somer; I couldn't take that place for too long. Standing over untrimmed pounds of weed. A bunch of mid, at best. Scraping caked on resin off my fingertips. Waking up at the crack of dawn to freeze my ass off. I didn't even like any of the strains we were trimming. I pocketed some to make up for my resentment anyway and got the fuck back to L.A.

  I don't know what I was thinking; everybody knows that L.A. is the capital of the O.G. market. At this point, I'd been on an OG Kush diet since 2007. My two weeks up north felt like four. It didn't take much, but I had my fill of the weed industry. It was as close to manual labor as I wanted to get. Emptying buckets of bud. The people were more or less interesting burn-outs. I ended up spending half my time lathering my trimmers with coconut oil so they wouldn't stick and the other half talking to the rest of the staff about conspiracy theories I could care less about. I took the train back to L.A.

I always liked taking the train up and down the coast because it gave me time to write. The scenic route was slow as hell. But slow meant more time, and to a writer, it's everything. Not to mention the beauty, it was fucking beautiful. The ocean as far as the eye can see and all that cliche shit you see on postcards. I fingered through my notes and realized I didn't have much. Not enough for a concrete narrative; I needed more, so I called my girl Paulette. She was grandfathered into the weed industry. The baby sister of two master growers, Phil and Payaso, and now the CEO of their collective and grow. Both brothers did an uncomfortable amount of time behind bars for their love of weed and lived to tell about it. That's where I came in.

Phil wanted a documentary written about them. We planned on calling it The Cannabis Brothers. Somewhere between getting to the grow and leaving the grow, a million other projects stole my time: strain descriptions, website content, contract drafting. Basic bud business shit, glorified copywriting, nothing too exciting, but it paid the bills. The only problem was, I convinced myself I was a useful trimmer, and the guys in the trim room gassed me up into thinking I could hang. Paulette discussed it with Joanna, who was technically the General Manager, but more importantly, another close friend. It was my first and only dance with nepotism, and damn did it feel good. Now I know why white America holds onto that shit until their knuckles turn whiter.

The next week I was in the trim room. They sat me next to this guy Jose. Everyone called him Toker. He was your quintessential cholo, or vato, or ese, or whatever slang terminology they say where you're from. Toker looked like a bald Benjamin Bratt with more street cred and less height. He was the father of four with one on the way and didn't seem to mind that trimming weed was his only form of income. "That shit is a blessing from God, fool," he'd say when any of the other guys congratulated him on the almost baby. Toker's favorite word and his most likely response to most shit was, "fuck". There was something endearing about him. Or maybe it was that everyone else was so damn disgusting that it forced me to rate them on a scale subconsciously. I'll never know.

Paulette was from a stereotypically big ass Mexican-American family. It seemed like half of them worked at the grow. Chito and Eileen maimed the garden; their sister Alexandra held down the office, her husband did the build-out and contracting. It was an all-out family affair, or maybe an Asunto de Familia. Most of the trim room guys were crazy motherfuckers Phil and Payaso ran with back in Pomona. Fuck-ups with records that had difficulty finding decent work. America's never given two fucks about smacking around the disenfranchised. Millions of brown and black kids all over this country are locked up in jail right this second for slightly profiting off selling weed. At the same time, white men are now doing the same exact fuckin thing on a much bigger scale and couldn't be farther from bars. This country is like a sore loser that keeps changing the rules mid-game so that it works out in their favor.

I learned the most about weed from Toker and Chito. It was a good thing, too, you really don't know how stupid you are until you learn better. Now I can spot boutique marijuana from a mile away. The expensive shit that makes you cough like a cowboy. I learned that the dry room where the plants hang should be so freezing cold that your nipples get hard. I learned about clones, moms, fenos, nutrients, terps, and some other shit that sounds like a different language, but is actually weed-related.

I'd set up shop with the rest of the timmers in that shit hole of a trim room by 6 am, and we'd compete for who could trim the most weed by 1 pm. Paulette's uncle had this bionic thumb that usually guaranteed him first place. Toker and I would battle it out for a close second if I were feeling ambitious. He'd usually win. He'd tell me crazy stories about his wife and refer to her as his lady because that's what Mexicans do. He'd detail all the dirt he's done and tell me how she'd kick him out and how she's just as crazy as he is.

[*dabbing/noun/ ˈdabiNG/ short for mid-grade weed. Vaporizing concentrated Marijuana, usually in the form of wax or hash, usually heated via blowtorch.*]

During lunch, everyone usually decided on a place and then peer-pressured one of the Gardners to go pick up the food. Toker was still opening up about his lady. He showed me his home screen on his phone. It was a picture of a tiny baby girl. "Iliana," he said. Toker went on to tell me that Illiana died and that his lady told him that the baby she was pregnant with right now was their rainbow baby. Imagine that? This tough-ass cholo almost at the brink of tears talking about a rainbow baby. I got teary-eyed, too. My period was around the corner, so it was only a matter of time. Joanna came over to partake in the smoke session and gave us our weekly weed allowance. Toker asked me if I wanted to do a dab. Like I said before, I still am and always have been a blunt woman. At this point, I graduated from backwoods to fronto, but dabbing was a different beast. The guys dabbed their way through the day, every day. They were built for it. I agreed to take one dab for the sake of camaraderie. Who could say no to a teary-eyed gangster Benjamin Bratt?

    Beskoe, the resident white boy, took out his blow torch. It was intimidating as hell, but cholos are like pit bulls, and they can smell fear, so I couldn't show it. Toker packed the bowl with some frosty butter, and Beskoe lit it up. I held the bong to my mouth and inhaled a monstrous hit. I couldn't hold it in for long. I burned creeping down my throat. As soon as the smoke touched the tip of my lungs, it all came rushing back out. I coughed for five minutes straight like a drowned victim on Baywatch. Just a lot less sexy. It wasn't the first time I experimented with dabbing. I took a dab at Paulette's wedding. Snoop Dogg and The Eastsidaz had a whole smoking set-up at the reception. It isn't a beautiful union en el barrio without a smoke sesh via Uncle Snoop.

Just because it wasn't my first dab doesn't mean it wasn't my worst dab. I planned on heading back into the trim room and taking first place since Paulette's uncle wasn't in today. Two hours later, I woke up on some boxes in the break room with Joanna's hoodie draped over me. When I looked at my phone for a time check, there were six hideous pictures of me knocked out and drooling in the group chat, above several snoring and cry-laughing emojis from the guys.

The next morning Toker came in with his left leg in a cast. I guess he had a rough night. Halfway through the trim day, he got a call from his lady that she was in labor. He was out the door in a matter of seconds. It was a blessing from God. We all took a dab in his honor.

Sixty Doves

"Life is what you make it, I hope you make a movement." -- Nipsey Hussle

It was Sunday afternoon when the city lost a part of our soul. Bible bangers call that day the Lord's Day. Shit, maybe it is. I was staring at a screen, waiting for my mind to turn on when I read the news. Rapper Nipsey Hussle, dead at 33 after shooting outside his store in Los Angeles. TMZ always has such a callous way of summing shit up. My heart sank. I had the same first thought as everyone else in this world. No, it can't be. It has to be a mistake. Nipsey wasn't just a rapper to Los Angeles. We have more rappers in this city than most cities have citizens. It wasn't about that. If I have to explain the polarizing impact of Nipsey Hussle, it's probably not for you to understand.

    To us natives, Nip represented a real L.A. nigga who loved L.A. and represented it, at all costs. He treated our home town as an extension of himself. It wasn't just some city he happened to be from. It was part of his being, like a limb. Nip never shied away from showing the underbelly of this chaos in a champagne glass of a city. A lot of the guys out here make you think that men with an integral code of conduct don't exist anymore. A dying breed, if you will. Nip refuted that by existing himself. He showed a whole generation of black kids that ownership, financial literacy, and nutrition are cool. He exposed the hood to a healthy lifestyle. An act in and of itself that single-handedly fought against systemic engineering. Now we have niggas in the hood running around, drinking green juices, and investing back into their community like it's gangsta. Maybe it is. But Nip did that. He led by example, and we were all better for it.

Bearing witness to everyone else's mourning was the only thing to distract me from my own. I called Asia. We were always each other's lifeline when something cut too deeply. And this cut below the white meat. We sat on the phone in silence before trading; I can't believe it's back and forth. She was texting with her mom, Gigi. Who had been debating whether she should drive over the hill to check on Nipsey's mom, Angelique. The two of them came up together like sisters, sort of like Asia and I. Granted, A and I have been at it a while, but Angelique and Gigi had a history that spanned longer than our lives. Finding yourself in someone and living out loud with them is one of the most rewarding parts of life in this material existence.

I couldn't help it; my mind wandered back to the internet to fish for information. It felt wrong to pry, but the desperation in wanting this to be a lie overtook my common decency. He was only thirty-three years old, like Christ. Conspiracy theorists loved that detail. He was shot multiple times, once in his head, another lodged in his lung. One bullet severed his spine, the county coroner would eventually reveal. The cunt that did this committed a sin against our entire city, a crime against humanity. Staining our soul forever. Rest in Peace Nipsey Hussle posts were flooding social media. A monumental outpour of sadness from anyone with a beating heart took over the internet like a tidal wave.

Pronounced dead at 3:25 pm. The first bouquet was placed on the corner of Crenshaw and Slauson by 4:19pm. Pictures showing a sea of bouquets and candles filled The Marathon Store parking lot monopolized front-page news. I didn't want to head to the scene of the crime with the rest of the city because I was scared that if people were performatively mourning it would piss me off. Take me to a place that I wasn't emotionally trying to go.

I walked to my car like I was on autopilot anyway. Passing my neighbor, Esme, coming down the stairs. In my personal opinion, she is one of our city's saviors. Always caping for the disenfranchised and underserved.

"Are you okay?" She asked.

"Are any of us?" I responded.

We had an intrinsic connection, and a soul as altruistic as hers was the only interaction I could handle. The smoke was still clearing from the fire of this l loss, and it felt like we were all in the thick of it. She went on to tell me about a kid in one of the programs she'd been working on. It was a work-study program for inner-city youth. She said that she'd been concerned because he's been pretty expressive about how motivational watching Nipsey's journey was. She said he lost his faith when we lost Nip. Not only in himself but in humanity and life. I'd usually try to say something to lend a different perspective. Esme and I played impromptu sounding boards for each other since I moved in. Nothing came to mind. I couldn't find another perspective to explore. Nipsey was stolen from us too soon, and there was no sugar coating or silver lining to be found in the darkness of that reality. All I could think about were the thousands of kids that feel the same way as Esme's friend. That an entire generation was robbed of an inspiration, Angelique, robbed of a son, and Samantha and Blacc Sam, robbed of a brother.

I drove to my local florists without even realizing where I was going. I just ended up there. The Colombian florist that I saw as often as one of my friends had a birthday, doctored up a bouquet of bright blue roses. It only seemed fitting. I walked to the ATM on the corner to get cash out for her tip, and the security guard muttered, "Gone too soon. Rest well, King Nipsey". I looked at him, smiled with half my mouth, fought back the tears, and put my hand on my heart. We didn't know each other, and we didn't need to. The whole city felt this like an earthquake.

Traffic was slow; hearts were heavy. It wasn't supposed to happen this way. We could all agree on that much. By the time I reached West Blvd. there was a traffic jam that didn't look like it would be moving anytime soon. It didn't anger me the way a traffic jam would on an average day. Everyone came to pay their respect, and I could respect that. Different tracks from Nipsey's Victory Lap album rang through the streets. Some were crying, others, ghostriding the whip while chanting

"Long Live Nip." There was a blend of mourning and celebration. Not celebrating his death, but his life. They were honoring his legacy. Waving the marathon flag and blue rags like they were pridefully representing their country—the United States of Nipsey Hussle.

I watched as grown men comforted other men with their heads cradled in their hands. I watched children and women pour out in hysterics. One young girl was repeatedly screaming "Why? Why? It could have been anybody else" before falling to her knees in agony. Faces were drenched with tears. Not the crying you could help. This was the crying where hyperventilating and snot are involved in the symphony of sadness. When you forget that there's a world around you because the hurt outweighs it all.

It felt like if the street lights could've shed a tear, they would have. Dozens of men from the nation in fitted suits and bowties were passing out newspapers commemorating our fallen comrade. Bloods and Crips that spent their lives fighting over territory were standing next to each other, paralyzed by the polarizing sadness. The energy that filled the air was equal parts disbelief, loss, and love. I parked my car near an old beauty supply and began to foot it. The traffic still wasn't moving, and bearing witness to everyone's reaction was evoking too much emotion in me. My eyes began to swell up with all the tears I had been fighting as I sat behind my steering wheel at a dead stop. Listening to Stacey Barthe's angelic vocals on Nip's last album only intensified the feeling. Marathon was about four blocks up. I parked my car where it was and began to walk.

The all-black Marathon truck was covered in roses and parked in the middle of the lot. An ocean of blue flowers overflowed onto the street. Bouquets of powder blue carnations, royal blue long stem roses, Sapphire Hydrangeas, Egyptian blue daisies. So many so that you could hardly walk, and more candles than a Catholic mass. There were mourners adorned in Crenshaw and Slauson shirts. People were waving the Eritrean flag, and full-blown murals had already been painted of him in great detail on the sides of businesses and on blank walls. A cop car had Nip In Paradise spray painted across the front of it. The only time I'd seen an outpouring of love for one person like this was when princess Diana died, and I only watched it on T.V. Real life hits so much harder.

A minister from the Nation of Islam began to say a prayer over the crowd with a megaphone. The crowd joined hands. No matter if you were friends, acquaintances, strangers, or enemies, we all joined hands and held a moment of silence. Sixty doves were released into the air. It was almost beautiful if it weren't so sad. At that exact second, when the last dove flew out of focus, I knew that the scope of this impact would likely turn into a before Nipsey and after Nipsey kind of thing. The next morning I woke up like the rest of Los Angeles did. There was a split second before I remembered everything that happened yesterday. A split second where I forgot one of our city's heroes is gone. I threw on Stacey Barthe, laid my head back on the pillow, and gave up fighting. The tears got their way. They rolled down my face onto my pillow. I closed my eyes and thought about those sixty doves soaring through the air of the Crip blue sky.

Horny For Likes

"Turns out it was mostly a lie. But, at least for a short while, it was a beautiful one." -- Russell Brand

If you've caught yourself staring down the barrel of a perfectly executed Instagram post against a pastel wall and thought, "You know what? Fuck them." You're not alone. The self-absorbed social media cesspool that we all swim in is overflowing with people horny for likes. Typically a little lust for attention never hurts anyone, but the problem is that no one cums. The proverbial orgasm that people are looking for by way of red hearts never fully manifest because there's no such thing as enough likes. Instead of getting off, everyone is operating in this desirous space that can only be referred to as social media blue balls.

To the untrained eye, these clout farming narcissists could appear like hashtag life goals. They are beautiful. They vacation and brunch. They perform acts of charity better than the rest of us, and they don't hesitate to post it. Hashtag Be The Change You Want To See In The World. The countless archetypes that fuel the socially fraudulent fire remind me of a national geographic episode that gives us an inside glimpse into the wild animal kingdom of fantasy and fabrication. It would almost be exotic if it weren't so damn predictable.

I have more friends that have sold their souls to The bad bitch archetype than I can keep up with. As expected, they belong to the bird species. Every time I refresh my feed, there's another facetuned cyber babe quoting Drake under a photo where she's looking back at it, with porcelain doll eyes. She's sunkissed, poreless, and perfect. Instead of feathers and toothless beaked jaws, these warm-blooded vertebrates have augmented, contoured cleavage, and blown out lip injections. Participating in such behaviors as unprotected sex known as cooperative breeding, clout hunting, and flocking around with other primitives. This bird is essentially harmless to everyone except their self-esteem. Often entertaining their hoe-phase after cuffing season. The hoe-phase is a natural element of the circle of life.

[hoe· phase/verb/ hō/fāz/ A a distinct period or stage in your life that frequently occurs when you are fine with exploring promiscuous activities and connecting with randoms. These activities do not always end in sex, but can lead to it.]

To observe a Bad Bitch in its natural habitat, you don't need to travel far. They are most likely found year-round in Atlanta and Miami. For those familiar with the West Coast, this species can also be found gallivanting at Penthouse nightclub, or in your favorite rapper's DM's. Should you lose track of this magnificent animal, they are often found in the winter season, migrating to the Dominican Republic for rest, relaxation, and plastic surgery on a budget. Hashtag Catch Flights Not Feelings.

So what does one do when their human friend transitions into a member of the Bad Bitch bird family? Well, don't do what I did. Don't go to another friend to ask for advice. I spoke to a mutual friend that seemed like the least judgemental confidant. I was sadly mistaken. It turns out, in the animal kingdom of social media, the person screaming that they have reclaimed their energy and that they are leading with love are most likely to be full of fucking shit. Case and point, my most recent conversation with The Inspirational Asset.

Next we have, The Inspirational Asset, the direct ancestor of The Bad Bitch, but better known as a parrot. This bird has the ability to associate words with their meanings and form simple sentences, as you can see in their regurgitated fortune cookie captions. Similar to chameleons, they are masters at camouflaging. Studies indicate that their uplifting captions camouflage the desperation for attention that their half-naked pictures would otherwise promote. Much like the pigeon, The Inspirational Asset is in every major city and small town. They feed on heart eye and crown emojis from other women and often use the eggplant emoji as a plan of attack as it is an unsuspected method following their innocent cooing. A historian that specializes in studying the Inspirational Asset was once quoted saying, "If you want to take a picture with your ass out, take a picture with your ass out, you aren't fooling anyone by writing some inspirational quote about God under it." Hashtag Protect Your Energy.

The Inspirational Asset had nothing inspirational to say about our Bad Bitch buddy. I reached out to ask her if I should accept The Bad Bitch's lunch invitation being that it had been so long since we were close. Instead, I ended up in a two-hour conversation about why one is a hoe and the other isn't. From where

I sat, it was hard to tell the difference, but the Inspirational Asset needed me to believe there was one. Do you ever notice that only broke people call other people broke? It's the same for women when it comes to sex shaming one and another. Only women that are insecure with their sexual prowess find space and time to shame other women over theirs. It reads pretty insecure, but I guess no one told them that yet.

"She's such a hoe. Did you know she sent Cam nudes?" The Inspirational Asset said about The Bad Bitch.

"Better her than me," I tried to joke to lighten up her mood.

"He showed me, and her body looks way different on Instagram" the asset went on to shit on The Bad Bitch. The same exact girl she makes it a point to comment "QUEEN" under all her pictures.

"But if she's a hoe because she fucked Cam, how come you're not a hoe even though you fucked him?" I inquired.

"It's different because he's liked me forever," she insisted.

The ground rules, loopholes, girl code, and laws of nature are ever-changing in the social animal kingdom. Cam was kind of cool but kind of a joke. It always tripped me out when chicks fuck the guys you're supposed to barely know. He was a bonafide club rat that probably didn't remember her name. But I kept that to myself. Recreational birdwatching is an important part of the ecotourism industry, and a creature that does it well is The Club Rat.

The ever-increasing population, long-tailed rodent known as The Club Rat is a Marsupial that often practices mating with the above-mentioned birds. The common creatures are opportunistic survivors and often live with and near humans. The problematic commensal species suffer from the fear of missing out and herd mentality. With their only two major predators being Party promoters and checkpoints, The Club Rat's average lifespan can vary. On a diet of Casamigos, various flavors of Ciroc, and champagne, they become sexually mature early on while reaching social maturity much later in life. Some have developed a diet for coke, molly, and antidepressants, and other drugs that deter this from happening.

While male club rats partake in nightly activities such as knocking down their female counterparts in the VIP section to stand next to a rapper, female club rats spend their evenings draped over couches scavenging for club photographers to snap pictures of them. The flash evokes a mating call at which they begin to arch their backs, pout their lips, suck their stomachs in, and stick their hips out. The female club rat is boisterous and proud. Their self-promotional screeching often attracts both the male club rat and various other nocturnal animals. They hunt in packs and howl at night. Hashtag Ended up at 1Oak.

Cam, the Club Rat, palled around regularly with Matt the Male Groupie. Both avid bird watching enthusiasts. Contrary to popular opinion, the Male Groupie, often confused for The Club Rat, is a sub-specie of the rodent family. It is the fastest-growing mammalian group native to the city. Several living subgroups are recognized, such as The Professional Best Friend and The Other People's Bottles Boy. This species holds a blatant disregard for anyone without a blue check next to their name, including family. Modern Male Groupies inhabit any events. They'll go to the opening of a fuckin envelope. Hunting styles consist of making themselves as accessible as possible to anyone with status and referring to men with clout as "Big bro." Practiced behavior includes social climbing, dick-sucking, both literally and metaphorically, and exclusively posting pictures of themselves with celebrities—hashtag brothers for life.

Matt, the Male Groupie, wasn't so bad, and he was a better sounding board for whether I was going to entertain a friendship with my Bad Bitch friend again. As mellow-dramatic as it sounds, before she was nip, tucked, and resembled a blow-up doll, she was one of my closest friends. Back when she was a human girl. That friendship went up in flames the day she kissed my ex-boyfriend.

"I was only hanging out with him to talk about you," she explained.

"Who asked you to do that?" I responded.

"I was just trying to help," The pre-Bad Bitch said while crying into her hands.

It's an interesting talent to be able to play the victim even when you've done the crime.

Crying is a lazy strategy that every above-average looking woman masters. It is assumed that the person on the receiving end can't stand to see a pretty face cry. Typically a full-proof assumption. This time, she missed her mark. I couldn't give a shit less.

    I cut her off without a second thought. I had a talent for doing that. Los Angeles trains you to take deceit seriously. It isn't something that needs several chances to prove itself. After so many years passed and the idea of dating my ex that she kissed felt more and more like a distant joke, we decided to catch up. It had been years; she looked like a Mexican Kardashian and was dating one of the wealthiest athletes in the world. I was still cynical, the way God left me. My immediate concern was being able to recognize her. I studied her Instagram like homework before meeting up. I asked Matt, The Male Groupie to sit us at the same table so I couldn't make any identity mistakes. He did. He and Cam damn near came all over themselves at her appearance. She always had that effect even before the surgery, but now she had a blue check, a legendary boyfriend, and a couple of million followers, and drove a Rolls Royce. It was all they could do not to piss their pants.

    We hung out that night and the next night too. Catching each other up on everything we'd missed over the years. She told me about how her lavish lifestyle was hallowing, and I told her I was still piecing myself together after my most recent breakup but that it was getting easier. Outside of the photoshopped exterior, she was the same girl. Still, a sort of sweetness about her: still, naive. I wondered if it was an act. I hoped it was an act. If it wasn't, that World Champion boyfriend of hers was going to shatter her.

    What she failed to mention was that he'd been on a fuck fest his whole career. Including the entirety of their relationship.

This guy was notorious for having a harem of women at his disposal. Buying them exotic cars and expensive bags before publicly humiliating them and demanding everything back. This guy was a class act. Although she knew him as hers, a lot of us knew him through Olivia, The Delusional Influencer.

It is difficult to identify whether The Delusional Influencer is trying to convince everyone else that they're famous or whether they're trying to convince themselves of it. They fail at both, but it is good to know where the effort is invested. However, the resilience of this creature is similar to that of a Camel because they tend to be expert survivors. The Delusional Influencer is known to be able to survive extreme conditions such as reality with an innate ability to create tone-deaf content and unboxing paid per post ads. They belong to the Public Figure Family of Animals. It's hard to take public figures seriously. It's not that I don't respect their hustle at working out, making gluten-free avocado toast, and showing off their skincare and travel blogging. It's just that I've reached my limit of how many times I can watch a pretty chick wash her face without falling asleep. Part of me feels bad for the prey that is The Delusional Influencer. The creatures are thoroughly convinced that they're celebrities. It's like when little girls dress up as princesses.

Olivia, The Delusional Influencer, had been fucking the champ six ways from Sunday. It wasn't her first time at a fuckfest. She's been known to dangle on the arm of box office action stars, and professional sports team owners. She's also the shady bitch that photoshopped the nude pics of The Bad Bitche's face on some porn star's body before sending them to Cam, the Club Rat. As Bad as the Bad Bitch wants the world to believe her to be, this one specifically is too sheltered to be bad. After Cam's mating dance with The Inspirational Asset, he gave her a private showing of the retouched photos. Cementing The Bad Bitches reputation as a hoe in the equally hoe-ish (if we're going to go there), yet judgmentally entitled Inspirational Assets mind.

Despite all this behind the scenes drama, an insect known as The Tourettes Emoji Commenter spams all of the above accounts with comments, likes, and private messages. Hashtag goals. Hashtag royalty. Fire emoji, Queen emoji, money bag emoji, bulls-eye emoji, marathon flag emoji. This parasite's oblivious nature is rather impressive as they possess a unique ability to disregard social cues both on and off social media. A mindless task they have mastered unlike any other creature in the wild.

It's an incestuous place, the animal kingdom of social media. Birds fuck rodents; insects stalk rats. But the jungles aren't only populated with overzealous rodents and attention-whore birds. Hypebeasts are running rampant throughout the kingdom. There is not one corner that is safe from them or their KITH sweatsuit. This animal can be observed in their native habitat, which often includes Complex-con, Art Bazel, & waiting overnight in a line on Fairfax avenue. They lack taste and feed on luxury designer streetwear collaborations. This impressionable creature uses an unsuspecting method of attack by pretending they wore a Jordan 1 before 2010, but really they overpaid for their footwear on StockX. This animal can also be found at social engagements for the purpose of riding the wave, alongside The Convenient Activist, fully equipped with perfectly lit pictures of them feeding the less fortunate or donating to a toy drive. With a heavy hunger for substantive messaging in their otherwise empty heads, they join in the socio-political conversations, oftentimes with their distant cousin, The Performative Protestor. While the intentions and messaging fall flat in both these species' missions, they continue to project their condescending calls throughout the animal kingdom. They feed on the attention that important uprisings like The Black Lives Matter Movement evoke, sleep with their makeup on, and never fail to remind you that they are hashtag woke.

  A lesser mentioned but always seen herbivore that is alive and well on all of our feeds is the Fitness Fraud. For them, it is always breeding season, and only the best bodies will be given a chance to mate. The male Fitness Fraud is not only narcissistic but also rather nauseating. Oversaturating our feeds with mirror selfies and ab shots. Hashtag results. While the female Fitness Fraud is often just a girl with a nice ass and a lot of spandex. This creature feeds on attractive people, pre-workout supplements, and before and after pictures. Unlike their notoriously known ancestor, the gym rat, the Fitness Fraud would have absolutely no interest in working out if social channels didn't exist and if their clientele were anything below a seven.

  I think I'll close out this educational chapter with the Look At My Money Man. This creature's natural instinct is to spend their kid's college tuitions on jet setting to impress random strangers. You may catch a glimpse of this beast out and about in the late hours of the night. You can recognize them by their bust-down chains and pretentious watches. Look At My Money Man is rumored to be overcompensating for their extremely inadequate genitalia and inability to please their female counterparts. Regularly, channeling their animalistic direct descendant, The Exotic Sports Car Rental Guy. Hashtag Humble-flex.

While all these archetypes do exist in the social media animal kingdom, I'm sure you can agree that it's no secret that they do not even begin to touch the tip of the iceberg. As we watch individuality and privacy suffer a slow and painful death, and this ecosystem of inglorious bastards continue to exploit our animalistic and voyeuristic nature, Welcome to the jungle. Tread with caution, like, comment, and subscribe.

This is America

"American history is longer, larger, more various, more beautiful, and more terrible than anything anyone has ever said about it." --James Baldwin

A few months ago, White America woke up and decided today will be the day that they will publicly acknowledge that systemic racism exists. I'm going out on a limb when I say White America because it isn't everybody. However, there is a sizable army of Proud Boys and White Privilege Princesses that beg to differ. I know this because a bunch of sister-fucking swamp dwellers stormed the Capital a few weeks ago in rebellion to our country tossing Trump in the trash. While the rest of the nation celebrated overturning a dictator. I know the white privilege princesses far better than I know the hillbillies for a pretty basic reason; She's my cousin.

I won't say her name because she'd love nothing more than to go into theatrics about defamation of character or loyalty to the family. I will say that when you're a mixed-up little monster with more nationalities in your DNA than you can properly identify, there's a fifty-fifty chance that you're related to a racist. Now she isn't all bad; there's compassion in her racism. The compassion is usually for herself and her white counterparts, but compassion is compassion. In full disclosure, I'm not even one hundred percent sure she's an actual racist. I'm nearly certain she's just one of those persuadable citizens from a targeted fly-over state that has been brainwashed and radicalized by the algorithm terrorists, Cambridge Analytica.

There really isn't much communication between the two of us, which I assume is how we both prefer it. The last straw was when I took a quick news contributor gig and covered the Black Lives Matter Movement for a culture hub. Every time one of my articles was published, it uploaded to all my social channels, including the dinosaur that is Facebook. Though this time, I was posting shit that said stuff like, "Another day, another unarmed black man murdered at the hands of law enforcement." Or, "You can no longer hide behind your idealism. The very existence of this moment proves your ideals to be misled and hollow." To say I wasn't intrinsically affected by this time in history would be a God damn lie. I've been Black all my life. I've loved and been loved by black people my whole life. And I'll continue to be black until I die. Probably after that, too, because the thought of existing somewhere as a soul with no rhythm or seasoning is far too bland a burden to bear.

You're probably inclined to think anyone with a pair of eyes should stand as an ally at a time like this. A time where mainstream media is finally covering the grotesque American tradition of blacks being slaughtered in the street by the racist cunts employed to protect them. You'd be wrong. My cousin had more important issues to address. The first being that the peaceful protestors were playing with fire and the news coverage was making her uncomfortable. This was when my not racist cousin took it upon herself to post something along the lines of, "I understand that people are losing their lives, but if these rioters come to the suburbs, they're going to find out why I bought my gun five years ago." I know what you're thinking, and ironically enough, she actually isn't white trash. Just another soccer mom in the middle of the country blinded by her own perspective. Of course, I responded with more turbulence than I typically would, but it was next to impossible not to be pissed.

I mastered the intricate art of ignoring my cousin's conspiracy theory rhetoric back when she hopped on the Crooked Hillary bandwagon. Another sinister mass manipulation brought to us by the fine folks at Cambridge Analytica. She wanted to see the emails. Even after the FBI released them, TWICE, and after the head of the FBI wrote a tell-all memoir detailing every nook and cranny of evidence, my cousin, Trump, and Giuliani weren't gonna let crooked Hillary get away with this. Not if they had anything to say about it. None of that has anything to do with right now. I said that to cement in that I was used to my blue lives matter, confederate flag waving my cousin. I've been ignoring her for years. The first time I did it, we were in the sandbox in her backyard, and she took her pale and shovel away from me, but not before briefly explaining why I wasn't allowed to play with it. You guessed it; it was because I'm black—an intolerable offense to a white-passing catholic school girl with sandcastle dreams. I didn't blame her or even hold a grudge. I figured she was just regurgitating some bullshit she overheard from some adults.

As much crap as I chat about being able to ignore my, our body, their choice, cousin. I have to admit I unleashed on her in a way I hadn't done before. I mean, I have in life, just never to her. She's always been sheltered and sensitive. Not just that, but every time I wanted to lay into her, I'd remind myself that she is to my mom what my niece is to me. It proved to be an effective solution until it wasn't. The fact that her pampered ass was bragging about potentially busting her gun was almost comical if it weren't so tone-deaf. The fact that she was doing so, in the midst of a global uprising as a response to police gun violence on unarmed black Americans, felt like she spat in my fuckin' face. If you think I'm one of those, know-it-all types that took it upon myself to point out the white privilege that comes with my cousin's "protestors scare me" perspective, you're Goddamn right I am.

   I machine-gun typed a response telling her that only poster children for white privilege complain about hypothetical threats to their property and disregard black lives. I tried to speak to the fact that she's a mom. She's got three daughters and a boy on the way, which I stupidly thought might salvage the sensitivity chip that's been missing for so long. It's probably an irrational notion, but I hoped the pregnancy hormones would have had some humanizing effects. I told her that coming home to find out your child or husband were killed in a routine traffic stop shouldn't be lost on her. I explained that her disposition comes across as racist and that as her cousin of color, I feel blatantly disrespected and would no longer stand for it.

   All she heard was the white privilege part. She went on to explain that she is exempt from white privilege. I'd never heard of such a thing, but I knew if I were patient, the explanation would find its way to me. And it did. My, I don't have white privilege cousin wrote paragraph after paragraph about how she's worked for everything she has today. She said she put herself through school and sometimes worked more than one job. She even went into some sad song about how getting knocked up by her teenage boyfriend resulted in highschool bullying for being a teen mom. Apparently, in her warped little mind, all of these truths exonerated her from white privilege. She was completely oblivious that none of her self-inflicted struggles had anything to do with the fact that she, and everyone she knows, have been coasting through life with white skin in a society intentionally designed for white people to thrive and black people to remain oppressed. It's the same thing as bowling with the bumpers on and thinking you're a self-made champion bowler.

My not racist cousin then pulled the wild card. She told me that I'm the real racist. My brother always joked that when a white person tries to pull the reverse racism card, it's like finding the golden ticket. Only all I won was a divided family. Because now I'm the bitchy big black wolf, and she's the soft sweet sheep victimized by the truth. Honesty has always had a habit of falling out of my mouth. My not racist cousin did what all well informed and well-intentioned family members do after an educational discourse. She blocked me right before campaigning to the rest of my out of town family that I'm the bad guy.

Within an hour of her blocking me, I got a call from our Aunt. She put on her tights and leotard and caped for my not racist cousin. Reiterating that she's hardworking and was once a teen mom. My Aunt carried on to tell me that she'd feel more comfortable if I advocated for white rights as much as I advocate for black rights. If I thought she had the intellectual capacity to grasp the truth, I would have told it to her. She was mid-rant and now focusing on my lack of patriotism and how it's a disappointment to my dead grandparents. All I could think about while she was committing to the role of ignorant Aunt was that she used to be friends with Gil Scott Heron. She'd told me stories about him my whole life. I find it hard to believe any of her All Lives Matter attitude ever reared its ugly head around him. What makes me different? I wondered if it was simply because she was comfortable enough to speak her truth. That realization hurt worse than her telling me that my recently deceased grandma would be ashamed of me.

    The only thing I had going for me at that moment was that I knew she was absolutely full of shit. I told her that when we all live in an alternate universe where white people are oppressed, I'll advocate for them. She said I was disgracing my Scottish ancestors. It didn't make much of a difference to me. I didn't even know I was Scottish. She then inquired as to why I don't advocate for Spanish or Native American people,. Sheattempted to drill into my head that I'm shitting on every other nationality that took part in making me beside the black part. I patiently and probably condescendingly informed her that I have advocated for both indigenous and Latino rights several times for several issues over several years. I felt stupid explaining myself to someone so committed to misinterpreting me. I even quite specifically gave her tangible evidence. Articles I'd written on the topics and photos that friends posted of us peacefully protesting. With a blatant disregard for every word that left my mouth, my Aunt graduated from unexpected ignorance to a basic ass pity party. Her closing statement was to let me know that I only care about the black community so I can appear "cool" because it's trendy. This left me with only two options. One, curse her out and remind her that her brother in law, nephew, and niece have been discussing and directly affected by this trendsetting issue for as long as we've been alive. Or two, hang up on her and end this vicious cycle of nonsense. Instead, I told her I was held down at gunpoint just a few months prior for running a stop sign. I hadn't told many people. Outside of my boyfriend and Asia, but this seemed like an appropriate time to bring it up. I asked if her if she knew what it felt like to lay on the ground with a barrel to her back, praying that the officer on the other side of it woke up on the right side of the bed. I thought that if my niece ever told me that she feared for her life, well, that would change everything. My Aunt had an impeccable talent for listening to talk. Everything I said rolled right off her back. I told her I loved her, but that this conversation changed me and I hung up. Shit, maybe I can go high when they go low.

    Some days later, I messaged both my cousin and Aunt to apologize. I didn't necessarily want to, but my mom was pretty adamant about the fact that I didn't consider what they'd been through or were going through. Turns out, what I've been through isn't of any importance. I said sorry to keep the peace and because the weight of a guilt trip from my mom weighs about as much as a full-size SUV. It's funny, isn't it? My race, ethics, beliefs, community, family, and friends were insulted. The very real emotion that comes with being a second class citizen in this country was completely disregarded. And still, I'm the bad guy. I wish I could say I was surprised, but I've been here too long to expect anything different. Besides, this is America.

The Friends

"Friendship is the hardest thing in the world to explain. It's not something you learn in school. But if you haven't learned the meaning of friendship, you really haven't learned anything." -- Muhammad Ali

It's hard to make legitimate friends in L.A. and keep them. The geography is unforgiving, and most of us are creatures of habit that live in tight-knit social circles in our own little world. It doesn't exactly make for an ideal environment to find your new BFF. Once you've lived here your whole life and have lost more friends than you've kept, you learn to guard your heart. That isn't exclusive to dating; it extends into friendships, creative projects, professional pursuits, and a bunch of other shit.

Most of us learned the hard way to trust the people who knew us before we knew ourselves. Some think you have to choose between being a person with deep friendships or someone with superficial acquaintances. Natives have a fundamental understanding that, whether we like it or not, there's space and opportunity for both. You'll have pretentious party pals and people you can cry in front of. The difficult part is knowing the difference. Drawing the line and standing up in it. I've had the same group of friends for most of my life. We called ourselves "The Friends." At least, to each other. The women that feel more like sisters than friends, and men that feel like brothers. I guess a few of the guys feel like sisters considering they insist on having a coke bottle frame and sucking more dick than all the girls put together. But that's neither here nor there. Point is, these sickos have felt like home since the day we met. Maybe we're spoiled because we get to see ourselves in each other and navigate this chaotic reality together.

We gathered as friends do for a routine game night. E.J. volunteered his place. He was a 6'5 power bottom with an addiction to fashion and a hilarious one-liner locked and loaded at all times. If 2chainz was a sexually fluid stylist, with a six-pack, chick hips, and a ton of botox, he'd look a lot like EJ. I've gone to bat saying he's the funniest in the crew. I'll never forget that one-year Karrueche had us all wearing white for her birthday dinner, and E.J. said our pictures looked like the Mississippi Men's Choir. See what I mean? Locked and loaded.

Karrueche was there when I got there. Ruech for short. She's our token actress-preneur. Would we even be a group of friends from L.A., if we didn't have one? When we were young, I always wondered if we would be the only people that actually knew how breathtaking she is. It seemed like a waste on us. But the jig was up years ago. The secret got out, the world caught on, and now Ruech belongs to them. But not tonight. Tonight we guzzle wine, overdose on her famous chicken wings, and laugh our asses off at E.J.'s collection of solicited dick pics. She can go back to being famous in the morning.

Joey was next to arrive, and more importantly, did so with five bottles of wine. As much as I hate to admit it, Joey is the glue that keeps us all together. He came with Estefany. A Columbian skincare goddess with a soft heart and nice ass. We call her Fefi, and she was just a couple of steps behind Joey. A gentleman would have held the door for her, but she didn't come with one; she came with Joey.

Erin and Shawna were a few beats behind them. You know the friend that says the shit that most people usually just think? Well, that's Erin. I call her E.P., An overly-opinionated publicist. Similar to Joey, but not quite. You know, the same, but different. E.P. is a fucking jet setter. Not in a way that makes you hate your life. She manages a bunch of private jet stewardesses and is usually on a different continent every week. But tonight, she was in Studio City because it's game fuckin night, bitches. E.P. is to Ruech what Asia is to me. They've been going strong since kindergarten. A year from this night, she'll have a change of heart in her career path and shoot her shot at Public Relations. She makes it too. Kobe would be proud. A year after that, she signs Ruech as a client to the firm she works for. Among her roster of other emerging actresses. It's kind of iconic. The only person missing was Asia. Per usual. My almost sister relocated to New York for a couple of years, missing a chunk of these random get-togethers. By the time she moved back, it was business as usual.

Once everyone caught up and got a few glasses of wine in them, it was time to start the game portion of game night. We usually resorted to playing an R rated version of Heads Up! Essentially, just a twist on charades where you have to guess a bunch of shit. The person who brags about being good at game night can't be likable by any stretch of the imagination. Unfortunately, I'm that person. Joey and I regularly slaughtered the competition when it came to game night. Just another worthless talent to add to my collection of uselessness.

Jacob was the last to turn up. Which isn't all the way fair to mention, he isn't one of "The Friends" and probably wasn't technically invited. But he managed Ruech, at the time, and came around more often than not. I never had much of a problem with the guy. He was smart, which was tolerable. However, he did have a thing for saying raunchy inappropriate shit. Show me a money-hungry man in the industry that doesn't. It's important to point out; this was all before we found out that Jacob stole over a million dollars from Ruech. They've since severed their working relationship, and the only association we have with the guy is when one of her fans, D.M. us an article about their pending lawsuit. Outside of that, it's onward and upward. How Ruech keeps it together under such extreme circumstances, I'll never know. She's always had this ability to always choose grace. Even when the situation calls for a bat through a car window, she finds a way to handle it with class. Ruech is a total Michelle Obama. She goes high.

Back to game night. It was Joey's turn. The category was Hollywood Celebrities. Typically a lay-up for the celebrity cult worshipper, but this time the name he was meant to guess was one everyone assumed he'd never heard of. Dick Van Dyke. I was the only one in the room that knew he would be able to make the association to Mary Poppins. If I weren't in such a stoned state, I would have just screamed "Mary Poppins." Had I, it would have saved a whole lot of blood, a severed artery, and a 911 call. Before I could say anything, E.J. screamed, "Bitch, it's the male body part we all love most!" Without hesitation, Joey guessed, "Dick!" he screamed. We all fell on the floor laughing. Most of us did it safely.

It's going to seem random that I take this time to explain a wine glass, but we've come this far, so you just have to trust me. Most wine glasses are stemware—goblets composed of four parts. There's the rim, which is the top of the glass. The part that beauty queens and failed musicians rub their fingertips along and call it talent when it emits its song. Then, there's the bowl. That's the important part that holds the wine. The stem is the thin sexy little cylinder that leads to the base, which is that flat round part that allows us to set the stemware down on surfaces.

Okay, now that we have the semantics out of the way, let's get to the gore. Joey fell from the couch to the floor, collapsing on his wine glass. The base of it was now protruding from his calf with blood squirting out of his leg like a bad scene in a horror movie. Joey looked at his leg, then at me, and said, "Brenn, take that shit out." As stupid as it sounds. I got a grip on the base of the class and pulled. Joey screamed out in pain. It was lodged in there pretty good. The room nearly cleared out instantly. Karrueche and Erin ran to the bathroom in fear they were going to puke from all the blood. Shawna and Fefi were on the couch cuddled up together, with their hands over their mouths and their eyes wider than one of those Snapchat filters.

E.J. ran to the kitchen screaming, "Oh my God nigga, please don't get no blood on my carpet. I just got that carpet." As insensitive as it seems, he also came back to the bloody mess with towels, which did help. I wrapped his leg and applied pressure to control the bleeding. Jacob was on the phone with 911 and talking me through what to do. The towel was absorbing so much blood it was no longer white but dark red. I switched to a fresh towel and repeated the applying pressure regimen. The girls were still nauseous and watching through their fingers when the paramedics rushed in. They took it from there. I wouldn't see Joey again until I got to the hospital.

As you know, this wasn't the first time I was in the emergency room worried about my *gusband*. This motherfucker was a lot more accident-prone than we gave him credit for. Last time, he turned to me under the fluorescent hospital lights as he was being wheeled down the hallway and said, "I can't believe I got stabbed before you."

[Gus·band/noun/ ˈgəzbənd/ A gay friend that a woman is as close to as a proverbial husband.]

Providence Saint Joseph Medical Center in Burbank was the closest emergency room. I walked in and pulled the "I'm here for Joseph Ryan Lacour, he's my twin brother" thing again. We waited in the hospital room for a while and took pictures for Joey's Instagram now that the shock wore off a bit. I'm sure you're thinking, who the fuck would take a picture in the fucking emergency room? Joey would, and did. A doctor came in and said a whole bunch of medical terms that in American English revealed that Joey cut his artery. "Isn't that the worst thing? Don't doctors usually say, at least you didn't cut your artery?" I inserted. The doctor told us that a specialist was going to come in to determine whether or not Joey needed surgery. After talking to the doctor some more, getting some pain killers in the wine glass slayer, and a brief conversation with the surgeon, the friends showed up. Just as worried about Joey as I initially was walking into the hospital, it was a Saturday night, and all of us were piled on top of each other in the Burbank emergency room and wouldn't have been anywhere else.

  Surgery wasn't necessary. The wine glass shanking did leave Joey with a bolder of a scar. The wound was now stitched up, resembling a relative of Frankenstein, and was swollen to the size of a baseball. All this because I was too stoned to remember to say Mary Fuckin' Poppins.

Shit They Should've Told You

"You're not done with L.A. until L.A. is done with you."
-- Philip Elliott

'The city of broken dreams,' lure of fame and fortune can be intoxicating for those foolish enough to buy into it. My dad always said that wisdom isn't seeing things, but seeing through them. The sweet taste of success is available for the taking in L.A. although it usually comes with an expensive price tag of disappointment and defeat. If you've never cultivated an emotional armor for rejection and can't handle competition, this might not be the city for you.

It's hard to understand Los Angeles if you don't live here. If you can't understand the people who live in it then you might not ever truly get it. The real Los Angeles doesn't give a shit about who you are, where you went to school, or if you went to school. It cares what you do with your talent and what you create.

It seems like the powers that be tend to peddle an overproduced fantasy rather than tell people the truth about the City of Angels. It's more profitable that way and money talks. The truth is that millions of people in L.Alive broken and hollow lives devoid of any real meaning or connection. This city has a way of doing that to you and doesn't discriminate between the rich and poor, or young and old. It'll torment you by twisting hidden pain and by preying on your insecurities. Pick another place if your weaknesses have anything to do with substance abuse, materialism, lack of ambition, or sex, pick another place. Maybe a town with a little more mercy.

I'm not saying that you will wind up on the wrong side of sexual assault, not that there's a right side, although I will say that being the penetrated as opposed to the penetrator most definitely has to suck more. I'm not even saying that you'll flip off a freeway or find yourself face down in a parking lot with a cop pointing his Smith and Wesson at your back. You might not have to survive one of the biggest earthquakes a major city in this country has seen. And you probably won't be taught about multiple orgasms by an R&B chick turned Disney princess or work wild hours in a grow room with Mexican gangsters. I'm just saying it's all possible. It's a goddamn shame, isn't it? You go through all that shit just to find out that it only seemed random. All that craziness was supposed to happen. Meant to make a me out of me, and it did.

Don't come here thinking you might fail because you will fail. This town is filled with failures that kept trying until their defeats became a pit stop to their intended destination. If you come here and find it to be intolerably superficial or image-obsessed, you're not wrong. It's that too. The secret is to ignore the noise and find yourself. Trying not to fall into the vortex of an influencer or reality star and what their warped version of this place looks like will probably be half your battle. Their perspective is as shallow and one-dimensional as they are. The truest L.A. has many different moving variables. It's layered chaos in the most beautiful way syncopated jazz. You have to listen to it at the right time to hear its magic.

Cost of living isn't cheap and increases faster than the average income. Thinking outside of the box is vital. Multiple revenues are just as necessary. If you have zero hustle in your heart, with a hard-on for homelessness, head on over. We've had the highest increased percentage we've seen in years pertaining to the unsheltered, so you'll be in good company. Over 80,000 people went from homes to the street in the last year alone. They'll show you the skyscrapers on T.V., but they'll never show you the hundreds of thousands of people who live on skid row in tents and boxes just a few blocks from that skyline of pretty towers. I'm not telling you any of this to scare you away, but so that you realize that economic hardship is not hard to come by in a city that prioritizes money in the wrong places.

    It's not easy to drown out the distractions. You'll suck at it, at first. You'll worry about the wrong things, even if you don't want to be. A vast majority will strike out after many attempts and end up worse than when you started. There is a sense of pride and defiance that fills the air. There's an entitlement that comes with living here that convinces you that you deserve what you want, and you do. L.A is a town of chasers, creatives, risk-takers, and people in pursuit of something. Dreams, freedom, happiness, healing, or whatever else they feel has been missing all this time. Millions of people leave their hometowns, families, and friends behind in search of something only L.A. can give them.

    This city's rapid expansion goes hand in hand with the corruption of politicians, officials, and police. So, there's also that hill to climb. But all in all, if I had to rate living in L.A., I'd say it's a five-star, highly recommended experience. The weather is undefeated, and if you find the right community of people, real people scattered between the lost souls and social climbers, it just might be worth a damn. If you can handle that darkness between the sky paintings of sunsets, or think the Malibu beaches and the possibility of possibility are a reward well worth the risk, pack your shit. But take an early flight because traffic's a bitch and the bars close at two.

Acknowledgments

Thank you to this city that somehow still finds ways to force my cynical ass to fall in love with it. And to my tribe of Los Angeles natives. Thank you for giving me a place to belong. But even more so, for allowing me to have such incredibly talented motherfuckers to go through life with.

To my parents, who double as my best friends, thank you for raising me in a house with more books and records and global news than anything else. You created an environment that allowed me to find my purpose at a young age, and for that, I will always owe you one. If it weren't for your constant critique and unconditional love, and support, there is no way I would have had it in me to complete this book. It may have taken too long, but I love you none-the-less. Thank you for everything, the little stuff and the big.

Morgan, thank you for understanding me in a way that no one does. Sometimes better than I understand myself.. You made me better than I would have been had I not been your sister.

Biggs, you are quite literally the love of my life. You make everything you touch better, including me. Thank you for letting me read chapters aloud and drive you crazy with my neurotic narratives. Sorry for the mood swings and tunnel vision. Thank you for cooking dinner all those nights I refused to look up from my laptop. Your motivation and drive are so fucking inspiring it should be bottled and sold. I love you in a way that I didn't think I could, and for that, I am forever grateful.

Somer, your patience in editing this high-speed chase of a book deserves a trophy. It would be a complete shit show without you. Thank you for your brutal honesty, your insight, and your tainted sense of humor. I wouldn't want to go dick deep into Bukowski and Rudd Judd archives with anyone else. Thank you for challenging me to always dig deeper. You were right

Grandma Grace, I miss you all the time but feel you all the time, so it's okay. I tend to be an ugly writer, but I know it's you when the pretty poetic parts come out.

Thank you to my tribe of Los Angeles natives. Thank you for giving me a place to belong and for allowing me to have such incredible motherfuckers to go through life with. Thank you, Asia, for being my soulmate and sounding board often and always. Thank you for challenging my crazy with your crazy. I don't care what anyone says, including DNA; you are my sister forever! Thank you to Joey for the laughs and the memories. Thank you for believing in me on the days I didn't believe in myself.

Thank you to Raychel, and Sal; I will forever cherish you and the years that were ours.

Asia, thank you for being the little sister that I always wanted but that my parents wouldn't give me. Thank you for challenging my crazy with your crazy. I don't care what anyone says, including DNA; you are my sister forever!

Thank you, Joey, for having the memory of a goddamn elephant. If you didn't, I probably wouldn't have remembered half this shit the right way. Thank you for believing in me on the days I didn't believe in myself. And for always telling me when I'm stupid. You're a real one.

Dahlia, your existence has taught me more about myself, love, and life than you can possibly understand at the age of six, but I'll explain it when you're seven. I love you so much.

Thank you, Esme, Ecca, Trigger, and Jaclyn, for always being there when it mattered.

Thank you to my family and friends who suffered through me talking about this book nonstop for the last few years. You're on my Christmas list.

Shit, it's over.

I mean, fin.

IT ONLY SEEMS RANDOM

Made in the USA
Las Vegas, NV
28 April 2021